X-PLANES
PHOTO SCRAPBOOK

COMPILED BY

DENNIS R. JENKINS

specialtypress
PUBLISHERS AND WHOLESALERS

ISBN 1-58007-076-0

Item Number SP076

39966 Grand Avenue
North Branch, MN 55056 USA
(651) 277-1400 or (800) 895-4585
www.specialtypress.com

Printed in China

Distributed in the UK and Europe by:

Midland Publishing
4 Watling Drive
Hinckley LE10 3EY, England
Tel: 01455 233 747 Fax: 01455 233 737
www.midlandcountiessuperstore.com

On the Cover: *A special Ground Effect Simulator was constructed at Edwards to test VTOL aircraft, and the Hiller X-18 was the first user of the device (below). Data gathered from the abbreviated X-18 test series was used during the development of the Vought XC-142 V/STOL transport. Unfortunately, the Air Force ran out of interest and funding, ending the program on 18 January 1964.* (AFFTC History Office Collection)

At upper left on the Back Cover: *The Lockheed X-35 was a technology demonstrator for the F-35 Joint Strike Fighter that competed against the Boeing X-32.* (Lockheed Martin)

At upper right on the Back Cover: *The three Navy-sponsored Douglas D-558-Is did not use Air Force "X" designations, but nevertheless played an important role in advancing aeronautics during the late 1940s and early 1950s.* (Douglas via Mike Machat)

At lower left on the Back Cover: *The first engine run on the X-47A was conducted in the parking lot of the Northrop Grumman facility on 8 December 2001.* (Northrop Grumman photo by Tony Chong)

On the Title Page: *The Northrop X-21 was an experiment with boundary layer control that used a pair of converted Douglas WB-66D light bombers.* (AFFTC History Office Collection)

CONTENTS

INTRODUCTION

Let's get this out of the way right up front – this is not an exhaustive study of experimental aircraft. For that you need to pick up a copy of Jay Miller's excellent work, *The X-Planes: X-1 to X-45* (Hinckley, UK: Midland Publishing, 2001, available in the U.S. through Specialty Press, 800-895-4585) as well as Jay's upcoming second volume that will cover vehicles that did not have formal X designations. What this book is meant to be is a collection of interesting photos of the various experimental research aircraft that have been operated by the U.S. government. Some of these have carried formal "X" designations; others have not. Some have explored increasingly faster or higher flight regimes; others have not. Several were intended to be spacecraft; I am not completely sure what a few others were supposed to be.

The concept of an X-Plane flourished after World War II. In reality – until the advent of the X-15 – there were two distinct – but cooperative – programs, one with the Army and the other with the Navy. The extent of the cooperation is best illustrated by the fact that the X-1, developed by the Air Force, was powered with a Navy-sponsored rocket engine, while the D-558-I, sponsored by the Navy, was powered with an Air Force-developed turbojet engine.

When people think of the X-Planes, what generally comes to mind are the record-setting vehicles like the X-1 and X-15. In reality, most X-Planes were dedicated to much more mundane flight regimes, and there were only a handful of high-speed manned experimental aircraft, built mainly during the late 1940s and early 1950s.

The contributions of the high-speed X-Planes were questionable, and were the subject of great debate within the NACA and the aircraft industry. How successful they were depends largely on where you worked. The academics and laboratory researchers – and a cou-ple of aerospace industry designers – are on record indicating the contributions of the X-Planes were minimal. On the other side, however, many of the hands-on researchers and pilots are certain the programs provided solid real-world data that greatly accelerated progress in the design and manufacture of the Mach 1 and Mach 2 combat aircraft that followed. Trying to sort out the detailed story is nearly impossible.

For instance, the X-1 was the first aircraft to purposely break the sound barrier in level flight, but other aircraft were doing so in shallow dives very soon afterwards. The first combat type designed from the start as a supersonic fighter – the Republic XF-91 Thunderceptor – made its maiden flight only 19 months after the first supersonic flight; how much the X-1 experience contributed to Alexander Kartveli's design is unknown. The same thing happened at Mach 2. By the time Scott Crossfield took the D-558-II to twice the speed of sound, Kelly Johnson at Lockheed had already been developing what would become the F-104 Starfighter for over a year. Again, it is unlikely that the rocket-powered X-Planes actually assisted Johnson very much, something he would make very clear during later deliberations.

The results of the high-speed programs – from a historic perspective – are ironic. When first envisioned by John Stack and Ezra Kotcher, the primary mission for the research airplanes was to investigate a flight regime that the wind tunnels could not achieve. But some creative wind tunnel design had allowed those facilities to get to the flight regime before the X-Planes could be built. In the end, the early X-Planes provided a way to validate the wind tunnel (and theoretical) results. But the need to keep up with the ever-increasing performance of the X-Planes forced the wind tunnel researchers to continuously improve their facilities and methods.

The North American X-15 is probably the best known of the X-Planes, and arguably one of the most successful. The rocket-powered X-15 eventually went 4,520 miles per hour and attained an altitude of 354,200 feet. (NASA photo by Dean Conger/National Geographic)

The modern X-Planes are infinitely more complex, and the tools used to develop them have gone from crude wind tunnels to sophisticated computer models. But, in reality, things have not changed much in the past 50 years. There will always be a difference of opinion between the researchers who believe wind tunnels (and now, computer models) are more than adequate, and the engineers and pilots who believe the final proof is always in flying a real airplane.

The more mundane X-Planes probably contributed more. Lurking in the shadows of history, a surprising number of the experimental aircraft of the 1950s and 1960s were dedicated to the concept of vertical takeoff and landing. Others were prototypes of proposed production aircraft and missiles, while still others were intended to show the way into space. A fair number of them investigated specific flight regimes or advanced aerodynamic concepts. Then there were things like the Lunar Landing Research Vehicle that almost defy description.

The next 144 pages present what I think are some interesting images of the research airplanes – fast, slow, beautiful, and ugly – it is a mostly random selection. I hope you enjoy the tour.

As with any work, there are numerous people and organizations to thank. First and foremost are two old friends who contributed many of the photos presented here, Tony Landis and Jay Miller. In addition, my sincere appreciation goes to: the AFFTC History Office, everybody at the Dryden Flight Research Center, Tony Accurso, Gerald H. Balzer, Don Borchers, Tony Chong (special thanks), C. Roger Cripliver, Colin Fries at the NASA History Office, Steve Garber at the NASA History Office, Dr. Michael H. Gorn at DFRC, Matt Graham, Dr. Roger D. Launius at the National Air and Space Museum, Denny Lombard at Lockheed Skunk Works, Michael J. Lombardi at the Boeing Archives, Mrs. Betty J. Love, Scott Lowther, Mike Machat at Wings/Air Power, Mike Moore at Lockheed, Claude Morse at AEDC, Doug Nelson at the AFFTC Museum, Ken Neubeck, Jane Odom at the NASA History Office, Terry Panopalis, Quentin Schwinn at Glenn Research Center, Chad Slattery, Emma Underwood at AEDC, and Dr. James Young in the AFFTC History Office.

Dennis R. Jenkins
Cape Canaveral, Florida

HIGH-SPEED FLIGHT

The X-1 was powered by a single four-chamber Reaction Motors XLR11-RM-3 rocket engine that burned liquid oxygen and diluted ethyl alcohol. The fumes are oxygen vapors. (Jay Miller Collection)

Initial unpowered X-1 testing was done at Pinecastle Army Air Field, Florida (later McCoy AFB, and now Orlando International Airport). The X-1 is in its loading pit awaiting its B-29. (Don Borchers Collection)

Not all the X-1 concepts used straight wings. Here is an X-1 with forward swept wings in one of the low-speed wind tunnels at the NACA Langley Aeronautic Laboratory. (Jay Miller Collection)

Two of the X-1s at Muroc (now Edwards AFB) South Base on 18 June 1947. The pit allowed the B-29 carrier aircraft to be towed over the X-1 for loading. (AFFTC History Office Collection)

Initially designated the XS-1, (the S, which stood for Supersonic, was also used by the X-2, but was dropped early in the program), the X-1 was the first aircraft given an "X" designation, and became the first aircraft to exceed the speed of sound in controlled level flight on 14 October 1947. On this flight, the first X-1 (nicknamed Glamorous Glennis) was piloted by Captain Charles E. "Chuck" Yeager, who achieved 700 mph (Mach 1.06) at approximately 45,000 feet. Beginning a precedent that survives to this day, the X-1 was air-launched – in this case carried under a Boeing B-29 Superfortress to an altitude of approximately 20,000 feet. The first X-1 is on permanent display in the National Air and Space Museum in Washington, DC. The second X-1, configured as the X-1E, is on display in front of the NASA Dryden Flight Research Center. The third X-1 was destroyed in an accident on 9 November 1951 at Edwards AFB, California.

The pit that had been used to load the X-1s into the carrier aircraft on South Base (and Pinecastle) proved to be less than ideal. By the early 1950s, hydraulic lifts had been installed that raised the carrier aircraft so the research airplane could be towed under it. This is the third X-1 (46-064) being loaded into the EB-50A (46-006) on 9 November 1951, the day before it was lost. (NASA Dryden Flight Research Center)

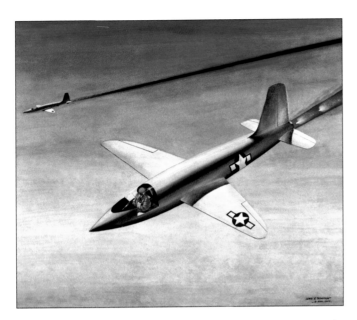

This is how an artist envisioned the XS-1 concept in late 1944. The overall design of the aircraft was not that different from what was eventually built. Initially, the NACA did not favor the rocket-powered approach to high-speed, preferring to use jet power like the Douglas D-558. The Air Force, however, was in more of a hurry and pressed on with the rocket program. (AFFTC History Office Collection)

The first carrier aircraft assigned to the X-1 program was a Boeing B-29-96-BO (45-21800) shown here with its original black-bottom paint scheme. After the aircraft went through major maintenance it lost the paint and spent the rest of its career in natural metal. This aircraft would carry the first two X-1s, X-1A, X-1B, and the X-1E. (AFFTC History Office)

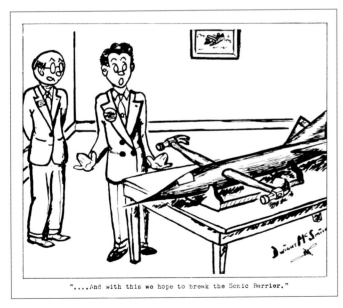

"....And with this we hope to break the Sonic Barrier."

Humor from the mid-1940s. (NASA History Office)

As delivered from the Bell factory, the X-1A wore an orange paint scheme very similar to the original X-1s. The aircraft was never flown this way, and spent its entire flight career in the natural metal scheme shown at the top of the next page. (Jay Miller Collection)

The second-generation X-1s were designed to double the speed of sound and explore altitudes in excess of 90,000 feet. The X-1A and X-1B made the bulk of the flights. The X-1C, which was designed to test high-speed armaments, was cancelled before completion. The X-1D was destroyed during what was to be its first powered flight. Possibly the most famous flight of the second generation X-1 series was on 12 December 1954 with Chuck Yeager at the controls of the X-1A. While flying at Mach 2.44 and 75,000 feet, the aircraft developed a slight left roll, but when Yeager attempted to correct, the aircraft snapped to the right and began a violent tumble toward Earth. Yeager was rendered unconscious from being tossed about in the cockpit, and the aircraft continued out of control until he regained consciousness and recovered at approximately 25,000 feet, an early example of the inertial coupling phenomenon. The X-1A was destroyed after it was jettisoned following an in-flight explosion over Edwards AFB on 8 August 1955. The X-1B is on permanent display at the Air Force Museum in Dayton, Ohio.

A rare photo of the X-1A in powered flight. The photo plane must have been in exactly the right place since there is no possibility it was actually flying formation with the rocket-powered X-1A. (AFFTC History Office Collection)

Initially, none of the original or second generation X-1s had ejection seats. This was rectified when NACA took over the flight program. This frame was taken from 16mm color film of the X-1A ejection seat tests during April 1955. (NASA Dryden Flight Research Center)

The X-1D at the Bell plant in Buffalo, New York. Its only glide flight was on 24 July 1951 at Edwards. The aircraft suffered an Ulmer leather-caused explosion preparing for its first powered flight on 22 August 1951 and was jettisoned from its B-29. (Jay Miller Collection)

The unhappy ending for the X-1A. On 8 August 1955, Joe Walker was at the controls on the second NACA-sponsored research mission when an explosion wracked the X-1A while it was tucked in the bomb bay of its B-29 carrier aircraft. Walker escaped back into the bomber, but attempts to save the X-1A were unsuccessful and the wreckage was jettisoned over the desert. Although unknown at the time, the third X-1, X-1A, X-1D, and second X-2 were all lost to the same cause. The propellant tanks on these aircraft were sealed with a product known as Ulmer leather; unfortunately, the chemicals used to cure the leather became very impact sensitive when exposed to liquid oxygen, and in at least these four cases, exploded. (NASA Dryden Flight Research Center)

The last three X-1B missions were flown with extended wingtips and a rudimentary peroxide-propellant reaction control system. This photo was taken on 30 July 1958. After the X-1B was grounded due to cracks in its liquid oxygen tank, the RCS system was removed and installed on the JF-104A. (NASA Dryden Flight Research Center)

A staged photo of the X-1B at the NACA Langley Aeronautical Laboratory on 15 December 1954. In early December 1954, the X-1B was sent to Langley to have instrumentation installed in it. Ultimately, the effort would take nearly eight months, and the airplane did not return to Edwards until August 1955. (NASA Langley Research Center)

Despite the loss of the third X-1 and the X-1D, a requirement still existed for a higher-performance X-1 so that the NACA could continue high-speed research. To satisfy this requirement, the second X-1 was almost completely rebuilt and redesignated the X-1E. Significant modifications include an updated canopy, ultra-thin wings (4 percent thickness/chord ratio), and a rocket-assisted ejection seat. The maximum altitude achieved by the X-1E was over 75,000 feet, and the top speed was Mach 2.24 (1,450 mph). An improved Reaction Motors XLR11, using a low-pressure turbopump, was also validated during X-1E test flights. The aircraft was retired from service in November 1956 after 26 flights, and is now on permanent display in front of the NASA Dryden Flight Research Center.

The X-1D attached to its EB-50D carrier aircraft on what is likely its last flight on 22 August 1951. The frost around the liquid oxygen tanks points to a powered flight, and the research airplane was destroyed by an explosion while its carrier aircraft was climbing to launch altitude on its first attempt. (AFFTC History Office Collection)

The X-1E on the lakebed at Edwards on 12 August 1955. Note the NACA band on the tail. (NASA Dryden Flight Research Center)

A large model of the X-1E being built at the NACA Langley Aeronautical Laboratory. The Hampton, Virginia, laboratory conducted wind tunnel and analytical tests that were compared with flight test results from Muroc/Edwards. (NASA Langley Research Center)

The second X-1 was completely disassembled during its conversion to the X-1E. Here is the forward fuselage during a test of the X-1E ejection seat on 6 April 1954. The natural metal areas correspond to the original glazed area on the X-1. (NASA Dryden Flight Research Center)

Depicted – incorrectly – as being the Kennedy Space Center on the "I Dream of Jeannie" television show, the X-1E is actually on a pole in front of NASA Dryden Flight Research Center at Edwards. Here it is with a rainbow in April 1998. (NASA Dryden Flight Research Center)

Usually overlooked when X-Planes are discussed, the three Navy-sponsored Douglas D-558-Is did not use Air Force "X" designations, but nevertheless played an important role in advancing aeronautics during the late 1940s and early 1950s. In the public's mind, much of the research performed by the D-558-I Skystreaks was quickly over-shadowed by Chuck Yeager's supersonic flight in the X-1. Nevertheless, the Skystreak performed an important role in aero-nautical research by flying for extended periods of time at transon-ic speeds, complementing the X-1 that flew for a few seconds at supersonic speeds. The three D-558-I Skystreaks were turbojet-pow-ered aircraft that took off from the ground under their own power. The first aircraft is on display at the Naval Aviation Museum in Pensacola, Florida. The second D-558-I crashed on 3 May 1948, killing NACA pilot Howard C. Lilly. The third Skystreak is owned by the Carolinas Historical Aviation Museum located at the Charlotte International Airport in North Carolina. (Douglas via Mike Machat)

The later D-558-IIs would initially be jet-powered (note the air intake just behind the nose gear in the photo at right), but would ultimate-ly follow the X-1's lead by using rocket propulsion and being air-launched (above). On 20 November 1953 test pilot A. Scott Crossfield would become the first person to exceed Mach 2 when he managed Mach 2.005 in the second D-558-II. (right: NASA Dryden Flight Research Center; above: AFFTC History Office Collection)

The first two Skystreaks on display at the Douglas facility in Southern California. The D-558-Is were much more conventional airplanes than the X-1s and were capable of taking off under their own power and conducting fairly long research flights. The NACA had been heavily involved with the Navy and Douglas in the design of the D-558 and thought it represented the better approach to learning about transonic and supersonic flight. Obviously the Air Force disagreed. (Douglas via the Jay Miller Collection)

The jet-powered D-558-I did not look much different than a contemporary fighter, and did not perform much better either. Still, they were well instrumented aircraft and provided valuable information for the scientists. (Douglas photo via Mike Machat)

The D-558-Is were jet-powered and did not need a carrier aircraft. Here is a 1949 takeoff roll from one of the lakebeds around Muroc Army Air Field. As delivered the D-558s were orange, but were soon repainted white. (NASA Dryden Flight Research Center)

Yet another method to get an X-Plane under its carrier aircraft – use jacks. It is uncertain how many Skyrocket flights were jacked in this manner, but it certainly seems to work. The photo was taken at the NACA South Base area. Compare the markings on the P2B with those shown on the facing page. (Museum of Flight Collection via Jay Miller

The D-558-II test force in front of the NACA hangar on South Base on 17 January 1954 (left). Once the D-558-IIs adopted rocket power, they needed a carrier aircraft, so the Navy supplied a P2B-1S (what the Navy called a B-29-95-BW). The P2B (BuNo 84029, ex-45-21787) was named "Fertile Myrtle" and carried the NACA number 137 (right). (NASA Dryden Flight Research Center)

After the test program was over, all three D-558-IIs and the P2B were placed in storage on the ramp at the High-Speed Flight Station. Here they are on 25 March 1958. The first Skyrocket (right) is now on display at the Planes of Fame Museum in Chino, California; the second aircraft (center), which Crossfield used to break Mach 2, is on display at the National Air and Space Museum; and the third (left) – still jet-powered – is displayed on a pedestal at Antelope Valley College in Lancaster, California. (NASA Dryden Flight Research Center)

This model of an early proposed X-2 was tested in the high-speed wind tunnels at the NACA Langley Aeronautical Laboratory. This design would transition into the interim D-37 configuration, and ultimately to the aircraft that were built. (NASA Langley Research Center)

An X-2 engine run at Edwards South Base in November 1955. The adobe wall structure still exists today. Most of the early X-Plane programs lacked the grand infrastructure commonly associated with research programs today. (Jay Miller Collection)

The Edwards air show has always been special since it is a place to see the most advanced aircraft in existence. This is technically the second X-2 (although it has an earlier serial number, 46-674), shown at either the 1954 or 1955 event. (Museum of Flight via the Jay Miller Collection)

The Bell X-2 (46-674) being demated from its EB-50A carrier aircraft after its initial delivery to Edwards on 15 July 1954. Two X-2s were built by Bell Aircraft at its Niagara Falls, New York, facility. The airframes were composed primarily of stainless steel and "K-Monel," an advanced lightweight heat-resistant steel alloy. Like the X-1, the X-2 was air launched, this time from a Boeing B-50 bomber. The troublesome and very short X-2 flight program proved to be somewhat unsuccessful. The first X-2 was dropped into Lake Ontario on 12 May 1953 following an explosion and fire that also caused extensive damage to the EB-50A carrier aircraft. The second X-2 was lost in a crash on 27 September 1956 after setting an unofficial world speed record of Mach 3.196. The aircraft experienced "inertia coupling" resulting in complete loss of control – pilot Milburn Apt was killed in the accident. No examples of the X-2 survive. (AFFTC History Office Collection)

The X-2 was an extremely advanced vehicle, and was equipped with a separable nose to allow the pilot to escape without ejecting. Unfortunately, it did not help Milburn Apt during the last X-2 flight. The "Starbuster" logo on the nose was only carried for a brief period. (Jay Miller Collection)

The Curtiss-Wright XLR25-CW-1 that powered the X-2 could be throttled between 2,500 and 15,000-lbf. The upper chamber was rated at 5,000 lbf, while the lower chamber produced up to 10,000 lbf. This photo shows the nozzle extensions used during the final six X-2 flights. (Bob Rohrer Collection via the AFFTC History Office)

The X-2 had a tragic flight program. The first aircraft completed (46-675) made three flights at Edwards, but was jettisoned into Lake Ontario on 12 May 1953 following an explosion and fire that also extensively damaged its EB-50A-5-BO (46-011) carrier aircraft. The other X-2 (46-674) made 20 flights at Edwards, the last of which cost Captain Milburn Apt his life when the aircraft went out of control after setting a speed record of Mach 3.196 on 27 September 1956. At left is the X-2 crash site. On the right is the X-2 wreckage in the NACA calibration hangar on 21 November 1956 during the accident investigation. (left: Jay Miller Collection; right: NASA Dryden Flight Research Center)

The X-2 underneath its EB-50D on 3 August 1956. Iven Kincheloe would take the X-2 to Mach 2.58 and 87,750 feet after he was released from the carrier aircraft. A month later Kinch would take the X-2 to an altitude record of 126,200 feet. (Jay Miller Collection)

A very unusual shot of the X-2 in flight, possibly on Flight 9 or 10. Of the 20 flights made by the airplane, only one made it past Mach 3, and three others were above Mach 2. For a program with such high hopes, it was a terrible disappointment. (Jay Miller Collection)

The X-2 under its EB-50D-95-BO (48-096) carrier aircraft in June 1952. (AFFTC History Office Collection)

The Douglas X-3 Stiletto was a radical departure from the X-1 and X-2 rocket-planes, and is probably one of the fastest looking aircraft ever designed. The X-3 was jet powered and used conventional take-off and landing methods instead of being air launched. Two X-3s were ordered. However, due to limited funding, lack of expected performance, and on-going engine difficulties, only one was completed – the second was used for spare parts. As a high-speed research aircraft, the X-3 was unquestionably a failure. It did, however, contribute somewhat to the understanding of the roll-coupling phenomenon, and pioneered the short-span low-aspect ratio wing used on several later aircraft such as the Lockheed F-104. But the X-3's most significant contribution may have been in the field of aircraft landing gear, namely the tires. Because of the small wings, take-off and landing speeds were very high (260 mph for takeoff, 200 mph for landing), and it was common for the tires to come apart. Several aircraft tire manufactures used data gathered by the X-3 when developing new tires for high-speed applications. The X-3 is currently on display at the Air Force Museum at Wright-Patterson AFB, Ohio.

The X-3 was hauled over public roads from the Douglas factory in Santa Monica, California, to Edwards on a flatbed trailer. This is the airplane being loaded onto the trailer on 25 May 1956 at the completion of the flight program. (NASA Dryden Flight Research Center)

This gives an indication of the size of the X-3 compared with a North American F-86 Sabre. Despite its sleek appearance, the X-3 was not appreciably faster than the F-86. (AFFTC History Office Collection)

NACA test pilot Joe Walker (in flight suit) talks with the ground crew around the X-3 on 23 May 1956 after the airplane's last flight. NASA Dryden Flight Research Center)

An odd view of the X-3 cockpit from the bottom looking up. Like the F-104, the X-3 was equipped with a downward-firing ejection seat, which has been removed in this 1 June 1954 photo. Unusual for a high-performance aircraft, the X-3 was equipped with a yoke instead of control stick. (NASA Dryden Flight Research Center)

That long, sleek nose on the X-3 housed the research instrumentation. The recorders and other instruments are shown outside the aircraft on 4 December 1953. Note the Northrop X-4 in the background. (NASA Dryden Flight Research Center)

Very few X-Planes had type names, but Stiletto seemed to fit the X-3 perfectly. The long fuselage and diminutive wings made the X-3 vulnerable to roll-coupling problems and many X-3 flights sought to understand the phenomenon. (AFFTC History Office Collection)

The two sides of the X-3. The top photo is probably at the 1956 Edwards air show – note the U.S. AIR FORCE marking, which came and went a couple of times, is missing from the rear fuselage. The photo above appears to have been taken at Wright Field after the airplane was delivered to the Air Force Museum. (Museum of Flight Collection via Jay Miller)

Like everything on the X-3, the canopy and inlets were designed for high-speed flight. Unfortunately, the two 4,850-lbf Westinghouse J34-WE-17 turbojets were just not up to pushing the 23,000-pound X-3 through the sound barrier except in shallow dives. However, at least 33 of the 54 flights were made using this technique, with the fastest reaching Mach 1.21 at 30,000 feet. (NASA Dryden Flight Research Center)

The X-3's roll-coupling problem had a silver lining – it helped fix the North American F-100 Super Sabre. On 27 October 1954, NASA test pilot Joe Walker was at the controls of the X-3 when he experienced severe inertia (or roll) coupling during an abrupt left aileron roll. After a few seconds Walker regained control of the aircraft and tried again, with the same results. Walker wisely elected to land. About the same time, the F-100A had experienced several unexplained accidents and the Air Force and North American were struggling to understand their cause. After reviewing the data from Walker's flight, the NACA thought it knew. After a brief series of F-100A test flights, the NACA recommended that two feet be added to the wingspan of the F-100 and the area of the vertical stabilizer be increased by 27 percent, effectively solving the problem and allowing the F-100 to go on to a very successful operational career. (NASA Dryden Flight Research Center)

The Lockheed X-7 was designed as a research tool for high-speed ramjet propulsion systems. A large data base of ramjet test results was generated during the course of a successful flight test program that lasted over nine years. There were four basic X-7 configurations: the X-7A-1 that was optimized for testing 20-28-inch diameter ramjets; the X-7A-3 that could accommodate larger engines; the X-7B that was similar in most respects to the X-7A-3 but was meant to test communications equipment; and the XQ-5 that was a dedicated high-speed, high-altitude target drone. In addition to basic engine research, the X-7s also tested various fuel additives and exotic propellant mixtures, such as boron-based high-energy fuels. At least eight X-7s and XQ-5s are known to still exist, including examples outside the NCO club in Sunnyvale, in the missile garden at White Sands, at Holloman AFB, New Mexico, at the Planes of Fame Museum in Chino, California, and at the Air Force Museum in Dayton, Ohio.

These photos are frames from 16mm movie film capturing various launches of the X-7. Note the lettering on the booster in the photo below that says "X-7 FLT. TEST NO. 19," providing a clear indication of which launch that frame is documenting. (Lockheed Martin)

X-Planes Photo Scrapbook

The X-7s were launched from a variety of B-29 and B-50 carrier aircraft. The total weight of the missile and its booster was in excess of 8,000 pounds, creating an interesting control problem for the bomber at separation. A typical X-7 mission used about 100 linear miles of airspace, with the X-7 reaching between Mach 2 and Mach 4 (the fastest recorded Mach 4.31) at an altitude of approximately 100,000 feet. The XQ-5 target drone proved to be somewhat of an embarrassment since its performance was generally better than the surface-to-air missiles that were being shot at it. (Lockheed Martin)

This X-7 is under the wing of a B-29-B-60-BO (44-84073) at Holloman AFB, New Mexico. Most X-7 launches were conducted from this desert facility adjacent to the White Sands Missile Range. Note the RATO bottles under the B-29 fuselage. (Lockheed Martin)

A giant lawn dart. At the end of a mission, the X-7 deployed a parachute from its tailcone and used a nose spike to dig into the soft desert sand as it settled at approximately 65 feet per second. (Lockheed Martin)

While much of the X-15 development work was accomplished in various wind tunnels around the country, other techniques were also used. Here a large-scale model of an early high-tail X-15 is being prepared for a helicopter drop to determine the design's low-speed flight characteristics. (NASA Langley Research Center)

The North American X-15 was arguably the most successful high-speed flight research program ever undertaken. The X-15 was constructed specifically to explore the hypersonic (Mach 5+) flight regime, along with the necessary structures, propulsion systems, and control techniques. Although widely discounted at the time, a secondary purpose of the program was to explore the possibilities of flight outside the sensible atmosphere. The aircraft proved remarkably flexible as a research tool. In fact, most of the later flights used the X-15 as a carrier vehicle for other experiments rather than as a research aircraft in its own right. An assortment of experiments were carried, including micrometeorite collection pods, missile detection systems, samples of insulation destined for the Saturn launch vehicle, and a wide variety of others. Before the end of 1961, the X-15 had attained its Mach 6 design goal and flown well above 200,000 feet; by the end of 1962 the X-15 was routinely flying above 300,000 feet. The X-15 had already extended the range of winged aircraft flight speeds from Mach 3.2 to Mach 6.04, the latter achieved by Bob White on 9 November 1961. Of the three X-15s manufactured, the first is currently part of the permanent collection of the National Air and Space Museum in Washington, DC. The second, in modified X-15A-2 form, is at the Air Force Museum. The third airplane crashed while returning from a high-altitude flight, killing test pilot Major Michael J. Adams.

Before the Air Force Museum, the X-15A-2 was displayed at the Alabama Space and Rocket Center (now the U.S. Space & Rocket Center) near Huntsville, Alabama. It arrived on 27 March 1970 aboard a Super Guppy and was displayed for almost one year. Note that the wing is missing. (U.S. Space and Rocket Center)

NASA test pilot Joe Walker in the cockpit of the X-15-3 on 17 January 1963. This flight would record Mach 5.47 and 271,700 feet. Walker would go on to record the highest flight of the program at 354,200 feet. The third X-15 was specially configured for high-altitude flights. (NASA photo by Dean Conger/National Geographic)

Rogers Dry Lake. Home of the Air Force Flight Test Center and the NASA Flight Research Center (previously the High Speed Flight Station, now the Dryden Flight Research Center). The original South Base complex is in the center of the photo, while the 15,000-foot concrete runway is left of South Base. The current NASA facility is at the extreme left at the end of the taxiway. Numerous runways can be painted on the dry lake and have proven a godsend to pilots of experimental aircraft over the years. (NASA photo by Dean Conger/National Geographic)

Getting closer. On 19 July 1963 Joe Walker made it to 347,800 feet on a training flight for his high altitude attempt. The target altitude had been 317,000 feet – Walker overshot by 31,200 feet! An extra second of rocket power could add over 2,000 feet during the climb. (NASA photo by Dean Conger/National Geographic)

Most X-15 flights took place in the morning before the High Desert got too hot for the crews to function. This meant that much of the preparatory work was done under the lights at night. The red cover on the nose of the X-15 is a protective shield for the ball nose sensor. (NASA photo by Dean Conger/National Geographic)

The X-15 had a side stick on the left console that controlled the reaction control system, and a side stick on the right console that could be used instead of the center stick if the pilot desired. Instrumentation was largely similar to other high-performance aircraft of the era. (NASA photo by Dean Conger/National Geographic)

The canopy is closed over Jack McKay inside the X-15-1 for a flight on 15 October 1964. This was the first flight with the wingtip pods installed on the aircraft. This was a relatively benign checkout flight, and McKay reached Mach 4.56 at 84,900 feet altitude. (NASA photo by Dean Conger/National Geographic)

An office with a view. The NB-52B (52-008), with an X-15 under its wing, prepares for a test flight while an engineer does the ever-present paperwork. The NB-52B would be long-lived, launching the X-43 on its missions. (NASA photo by Dean Conger/National Geographic)

The Reaction Motors XLR99 in the X-15 was the most powerful man-rated throtteable rocket engine built until the advent of the Space Shuttle Main Engine in the late 1970s. (NASA photo by Dean Conger/National Geographic)

The XLR99 produced between 57,000 and 61,000 lbf and propelled the X-15A-2 to 4,520 miles per hour (Mach 6.7). The XLR99 was a remarkably reliable engine given its level of sophistication and prototype status, but as a safety precaution it was test fired frequently in a special rocket engine test facility at Edwards. (NASA photo by Dean Conger/National Geographic)

The X-43A Hyper-X program seeks to overcome one of the greatest aeronautical research challenges – air-breathing hypersonic flight. The X-43A vehicles were intended to fly at speeds of Mach 7 and 10, and the goal of the Hyper-X program is to validate key propulsion and related technologies for air-breathing hypersonic aircraft. The vehicles were not designed to be recovered, and all data will be telemetered to the ground during the flight. The first X-43A and its modified Pegasus booster were carried aloft by the NASA NB-52B carrier aircraft from Dryden Flight Research Center on 2 June 2001 for the first of three high-speed free flight attempts. About an hour and 15 minutes later the Pegasus booster was released from the NB-52B to accelerate the X-43A to its intended speed of Mach 7. However, the combined Pegasus and X-43A stack lost control about eight seconds after Pegasus ignition; the mission was terminated by the Range Safety Officer, and the Pegasus and X-43A fell into the Pacific Ocean in a cleared Navy range area. The second X-43A was successfully launched on 27 March 2004 and the scramjet engine produced a small positive net thrust (more thrust than drag), a first in actual flight. The scramjet engine operated for about 10 seconds and slightly accelerated the X-43A at about Mach 7. A third X-43A flight is scheduled to validate the results already attained. A planned X-43C follow-on vehicle has been cancelled.

Things have changed for X-Planes. Here the X-43A is undergoing radio frequency testing in the Benefield Anechoic Facility at Edwards in January 2000, a modern necessity that never even occurred to the developers of the X-15. (NASA Dryden photo by Tom Tschida)

The first X-43 vehicle undergoing ground vibration testing in December 1999. The X-43A is essentially a subscale version of the planned X-30 National Aerospace Plane (NASP) and is the last remaining part of that program. (NASA Dryden photo by Tom Tschida)

The second X-43A flight on 27 March 2004 demonstrated that a scramjet engine could produce a small positive net thrust. A modified Pegasus booster took the X-43A to 95,000 feet and just below Mach 7 prior to releasing the research vehicle for its flight. The vehicle was carried aloft by the same NB-52B (52-008) that carried the X-15 and lifting bodies for their flights. (NASA Dryden photo by Jim Ross)

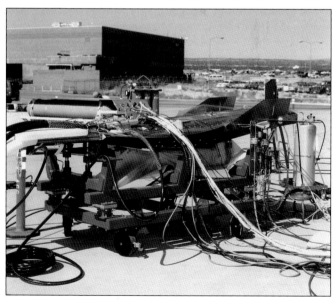

The first X-43A undergoing ground tests in September 2000. The vehicle was remarkably small, as shown in the photo at left with a man for reference. The program was initially on a fast track to demonstrate scramjet technology, but a variety of setbacks meant the third and final flight of the program will not occur until late 2004 or early 2005. (NASA Dryden photo by Tom Tschida)

The second X-43A hypersonic research vehicle as viewed from the cockpit of the NB-52B. It would take over 35 years for the X-Planes at Edwards to get from the Mach 6.7 recorded by the X-15A-2 to the Mach 7 X-43A. (NASA Dryden photo by Tony Landis)

The scramjet module on the bottom of the X-43A. Unlike jet and ramjet engines that require subsonic air, the scramjet supports supersonic combustion – it has been the holy grail of designers for almost 50 years. (NASA Dryden photo by Tom Tschida)

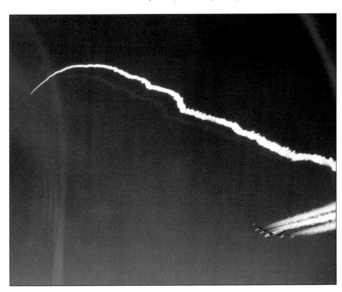

The second X-43A and its modified Pegasus booster accelerates away from the NB-52B over the Pacific Ocean during the second X-43A flight on 27 March 2004. (NASA Dryden photo by Jim Ross)

The X-43A project team assembled on 23 March 2004 for a group photo in front of the NB-52B and second X-43A vehicle mounted to its Pegasus booster. (NASA Dryden photo by Tom Tschida)

Above and below: *The NB-52B taking off from Edwards for the second X-43A flight on 27 March 2004.* (above: NASA Dryden photo by Tony Landis; below: NASA Dryden photo by Jim Ross)

VERTICAL FLIGHT

The Ryan Aeronautical Company X-13 Vertijet was designed to explore the feasibility of building a pure-jet vertical takeoff and landing (VTOL) fighter aircraft. The diminutive X-13 was powered by a single Rolls-Royce Avon turbojet engine. The success and efficiency of the X-13 flight test program remains a high water mark in the history of research aircraft and provided a significant amount of data to the designers of subsequent VTOL aircraft designs. The X-13s proved that vertical flight, on jet thrust alone, was both technically feasible and practical. The ease with which the aircraft routinely transitioned from vertical to horizontal attitude, and back again, left little question as to the flexibility and operational utility of such flight modes. Perhaps the only significant failing of the program was its lack of success in generating a follow-on production effort. This was due mainly to the aircraft's small size and limited payload capacity – and the inability of existing turbojet engines to power a larger version. Both X-13s survived their test program. The first aircraft is on loan from the National Air and Space Museum to the San Diego Aero-space Museum in California. The second aircraft is on display at the Air Force Museum in Dayton, Ohio.

Delivering the X-13 from the Ryan factory in San Diego to Edwards was simple – put the X-13 on a flatbed truck. It arrived, covered with a tarp, on 18 August 1955. (AFFTC History Office Collection)

The X-13 was tiny by any standard – only 23 feet 5 inches long with a wingspan of 21 feet. The airplane weighed 5,334 pounds empty and 7,313 pounds full-up. A single Rolls Royce Avon RA.28-49 turbojet provided 10,000 lbf. (AFFTC History Office Collection)

The first hover tests were conducted with a special tubular test rig attached to the X-13 so that the pilot could land anywhere, not just on the launch trailer. Note the access ladder extending over the vertical stabilizer to the cockpit. (AFFTC History Office Collection)

The second X-13 (54-1620) sitting on its launch trailer at Edwards on 9 April 1957. Using this trailer, the X-13 could be launched and recovered virtually anywhere, including parking lots and roads. (AFFTC History Office Collection)

The first transition flight occurred on 11 April 1957 when the X-13 took off vertically from its trailer, transitioned to conventional flight, then landed vertically. Eventually the procedure became routine, and the aircraft was even demonstrated in the parking lot at the Pentagon. (AFFTC History Office Collection)

The landing mechanism was deceptively simple – a short length of cable stretched across the top of the trailer, caught by a retractable hook under the nose. To take off, the aircraft increased power and unhooked. To land, the pilot entered a hover and slowly descended until the hook caught the cable. (AFFTC History Office Collection)

A conventional tricycle landing gear was attached for the initial series of horizontal flight tests. (AFFTC History Office Collection)

X-Planes Photo Scrapbook

The Bell X-14 was another X-Plane dedicated to exploring vertical flight. The X-14 was originally created to explore the feasibility of operating a vertical takeoff and landing (VTOL) aircraft from a normal pilot station using standard flight instruments and references. Of equal importance, the X-14 was to demonstrate various VTOL systems and engine technologies. The X-14 successfully demonstrated that the concept of vectored jet thrust was viable, as subsequently used on the BAe/McDonnell Douglas Harrier. Flight tests using the X-14's variable stability control system resulted in major contributions to the understanding of V/STOL handling characteristics. The X-14 also proved useful as a testbed for various unique V/STOL concepts, such as NASA's direct side-force maneuvering system. Over 25 pilots from around the world previewed V/STOL handling qualities in the X-14 prior to making test flights in other V/STOL designs. Numerous proposals for operational versions were stillborn. The single X-14 continued flying for nearly a quarter century before being retired to the Army Aviation Museum at Fort Rucker, Alabama. It is currently in storage at a private collection in Indiana.

In April 1953 Bell began the construction of the Model 65 Air Test Vehicle (ATV) to explore VTOL concepts. A Fairchild J44 cruise missile engine was swivel-mounted on each side of the fuselage and could be rotated to provide vertical or horizontal thrust. Eventually the skids were replaced by a wheeled landing gear. (Jay Miller Collection)

The ATV had demonstrated that vectored thrust would work, so Bell built the Model 68 to test a slightly more sophisticated "deflected" thrust concept. The X-14 initially used a pair of Armstrong-Siddeley Viper turbojets. (Jay Miller Collection)

The first hover flight was on 17 February 1957, and the initial transition flight was on 24 May 1958. The Air Force transferred the X-14 to the NASA Ames Research Center at Moffett Field, California, in October 1959. (NASA History Office Collection)

Within a year NASA decided that the major limitation of the X-14 was the limited thrust from the Armstrong engines. A decision was made to install a pair of General Electric J85-GE-5 engines, and the airplane was redesignated X-14A. (Museum of Flight via Jay Miller)

Instead of swiveling the entire engine like the earlier ATV, the X-14 used these Bell-designed cascading-type deflector exhaust nozzles to vector the thrust from the two turbojet engines. A cable system rotated the nozzles as needed. (Jay Miller Collection)

After 11 more years of flight testing at Ames, the airplane again received new engines, this time a pair of General electric J85-GE-19s, along with a new X-14B designation. A "hard landing" at Ames on 29 May 1981 finally grounded the X-14. (NASA History Office Collection)

The Hiller X-18 was conceived to assess the feasibility and practicality of a large tilt-wing V/STOL aircraft. The primary objectives were to investigate major problems associated with the tilt-wing concept while establishing criteria for the possible future development of similar aircraft. Although its flight test program was short and inconclusive, the X-18 was nevertheless the first large aircraft to investigate the tilt-wing concept. An engine failure on the 20th flight prematurely terminated the test program. Data from this program was used during the design and development of the Vought XC-142 experimental transport aircraft in the early 1960s. Only a single X-18 was completed – interestingly it used the fuselage from the Chase YC-122C and two turboprop engines that were surplused from the Navy's cancelled VTOL fighter program (Lockheed XFV-1 and Convair XFY-1 Pogo). No definitive information has been uncovered concerning the aircraft's ultimate fate, but it is generally assumed to have been scrapped at Edwards AFB.

The Hiller X-18 was the first attempt to build a large tilt-wing aircraft and made its first "hop" on 20 November 1959 and its first real flight four days later. (AFFTC History Office Collection)

Originally developed as a private venture by Curtiss-Wright, the X-19 was intended to demonstrate the practicality of the tilt-rotor concept. The X-19 was also used to explore the general feasibility of VTOL operations for such missions as the evacuation of person-

nel, missile site support, delivery of high priority cargo, counter-insurgency operations, reconnaissance, and close support operations. Within the limited flight envelope explored by the X-19 prior to its demise, the aircraft demonstrated the general feasibility of the tandem tilt-rotor concept. The program successfully verified the dynamic and longitudinal stability, hover, and transition performance of the basic design. Much of the data proved useful during the development of the XV-15 and later V-22 tilt-rotor aircraft and during 2004 Bell is again investigating a larger tandem tilt-rotor transport. Two X-19s were built – the first was destroyed in an accident on 25 August 1965, and the second aircraft was never completed. After all the useable components from the second aircraft were removed, the airframe was stored at the Aberdeen Proving Grounds and is currently in poor shape; it has been allocated to the Martin Museum in Maryland.

The second X-19 (62-12198) photographed at the Aberdeen Proving Grounds, Maryland, in April 1982. This aircraft was not flown during the test program. (Stan Piet)

The X-22 took a different approach to VTOL flight from the tilt-wings and tilt-engines – tilting ducted fans. Four General Electric YJ58-GE-8D turboshafts were mounted in pairs at the root of each aft wing and drove a complex series of cross-shafts such that any engine could drive all the propellers. (Jack Beilman Collection)

The X-22 test team after the 200th flight on 12 February 1980. Back row: Bob Harper, Ed Frantz, Jim Hooper, Dominic Andrisano, Tom Gavin, Bob Radford, unknown, Bill Wilcox, Don Dobmeier, Major Paul Wilson. Front: Mike Sears, Tom Franclemont, John Shattuck, Rogers Smith, Jean Oddo, Mike Parrag, Nello Infanti, Ken Burnham, Jack Beilman. The team claimed that the X-22 was the first X-Plane to reach 200 flights (finally beating the X-15's 199 flights), but it is possible that some of the "non-airplane" X-designations had already done it. (Jack Beilman Collection)

The first X-22A made its initial hover flight on 17 March 1966, and the first STOL takeoff was on 30 June; unfortunately, the aircraft crashed five weeks later (photo at right). The program's first full transition was by the second X-22A on 26 January 1967. (Jack Beilman Collection)

The aircraft was severely damaged during an emergency landing on 8 August 1966. The crew escaped unharmed. Repairing the aircraft was deemed uneconomical, but parts from the airframe were used to build an X-22 simulator at Calspan. (Jack Beilman)

A half-shaft test rig was built at the Curtiss-Wright facility in Caldwell, New Jersey to verify the Lycoming T55 turboshaft engine, propellers, and gearboxes for the X-19. All four propellers on the airplane were cross-shafted together for safety. (Jay Miller Collection)

The X-19 wore the short-lived "Tri-Service" markings that indicated the program was supported by the Air Force, Army, and Navy. Several of the X-Planes would be part of this early "joint" program. (Jay Miller Collection)

The first airplane (62-12197) was the only X-19 to fly, making its first flight on 20 November 1963. The aircraft was destroyed in a crash on 25 August 1965 at the Federal Aviation Administration's National Aviation Facility Experimental Center (NAFEC) near Atlantic City, New Jersey. Both pilots ejected safely, but the accident effectively ended the X-19 program. (Jay Miller Collection)

The first X-22A (BuNo 151520) was rolled out on 25 May 1965. The two X-22s were the last aircraft manufactured by Bell in its Wheatfield, New York, facility near Niagara Falls. The second aircraft (151521) would follow on 30 October. (Tony Landis Collection)

The Bell Aerospace Textron X-22A was intended to evaluate a unique dual tandem ducted-propeller configuration for a V/STOL transport aircraft. It was also, from the beginning, designed to provide a highly versatile platform capable of general research on V/STOL handling qualities using a unique variable stability control system. The flight test program was undertaken by Calspan Corporation, in Buffalo, New York, under the auspices of the U.S. Navy. After demonstrating its basic handling qualities, most of the X-22A flights were oriented towards advancing the science of V/STOL flight, not the specific aircraft configuration itself. By the end of its long-lived test program, the X-22A had made a number of contributions, but perhaps the most significant was its ability to serve as a V/STOL analog for various advanced sensors and instrumentation destined for other V/STOL aircraft. The ducted-fan configuration itself proved quite workable, although it has not been selected for any further aircraft to date. Two X-22As were built. The first was damaged beyond economical repair on 8 August 1966, and it was cannibalized to keep the second aircraft flying, although the fuselage was retained for a considerable time for use as a ground simulator at Calspan. The second aircraft is on display at the Niagara Aviation Museum in New York.

X-22 Program Manager Jack Beilman looks into the cockpit of the first X-22. Note the way the canopies open and the Tri-Service markings. The experimental program was managed by the Navy, and the two aircraft were assigned Bureau Numbers 151520 and 151521. (Jack Beilman Collection)

The development of the XV-15 was initiated in 1973 as a tiltrotor technology demonstration program. Two aircraft were manufactured by Bell Helicopter Textron in 1977 using Army and NASA funding. The first aircraft was given NASA number 702, and the second was 703. The first flight was on 3 May 1977, and the last test flight was on 11 July 2003. Data gathered by the XV-15s was used during the development of the V-22 Osprey, but several proposals for production derivatives of the XV-15 itself went nowhere. (NASA Dryden Flight Research Center)

The XV-15 was powered by two 1,550-hp Lycoming LTC1K-4K (T53) turboshaft engines that were connected by a cross-shaft and drove three-bladed, 25-foot diameter rotors. This allowed the XV-15 to record speeds up to 345 mph. (NASA Dryden Flight Research Center)

The first XV-15 crashed in 1992, but the second eventually completed over 800 flight hours and is currently on display at the National Air and Space Museum's Steven F. Udvar-Hazy Center at Dulles airport. (NASA Dryden Flight Research Center)

The XV-15 at At NASA Langley during 1982 in the markings applied for the Paris Air Show. (NASA Langley Research Center)

The Vertol Model 76 was designated VZ-2 by the U.S. Army and was an early tilt-wing research aircraft. (NASA Langley Research Center)

The Curtiss-Wright X-100 (a company designation, not an Air Force one) was powered by a single Lycoming YT53 turboshaft engine. the aircraft proved much of the technology used in the X-19 program. The first tethered hover took place on 20 April 1959, with the first STOL flight on 29 March 1960. The aircraft was extensively tested at NASA Langley in 1960-61. The aircraft was extensively damaged in an accident on 5 October 1961 and is currently in storage at the National Air and Space Museum. (Jay Miller Collection)

The Vertol Model 76 was designated VZ-2 in early 1956. A single 860-hp Lycoming YT53-L-1 was mounted on top of the fuselage and drove two 9.5-foot diameter three-bladed propellers by a cross-shaft. Hover control was provided by two ducted propellers in the tail, and aerodynamic controls were phased in during transition to horizontal flight. The first vertical flight was made on 13 August 1957 and the first complete transition on 15 July 1958. The airplane was retired in 1965 after more than 450 flights. (Museum of Flight via Jay Miller)

Oddly, the Vertol VZ-2 exhibited a "negative" ground effect. During descent, the aircraft experienced a sharp increase in rate of descent as it approached the ground; conversely, during low-speed ascents, the aircraft experienced a notable increase in rate of climb as it got out of ground effect. (NASA Langley Research Center)

Langley pilots posing in front of the VZ-2 in 1960 (from left): Bud Ream, Donald Mallick, Robert Sommer, Joe Algranti, James Whitten, and John "Jack" Reeder. Note the revised canopy compared to the top photo. The aircraft is currently in storage at the National Air and Space Museum. (NASA Langley Research Center)

The Doak Aircraft Company Model 16 was designated VZ-4A by the Army. This was the first VTOL aircraft to demonstrate the tilt-ducted-fan concept. The first hover flight was on 25 February 1958, and the aircraft was transferred to Edwards in October 1958 where it accumulated 50 flight hours. The VZ-4A arrived at NASA Langley on 5 May 1960 and was donated to the United States Army Transportation Museum at Fort Eustis, Virginia, on 21 August 1972. Doak, located in Torrence, California, was eventually absorbed by the nearby Douglas Aircraft Company. (NASA Langley Research Center)

In November 1961 General Electric won an Army contract to develop its fan-in-wing concept, designated VZ-11 (later redesignated XV-5A). The design and construction of the aircraft was subcontracted to Ryan Aeronautical, with GE supplying the engines and lift system. The inboard portion of each wing contained a 5-foot diameter fan that provided vertical lift, and a smaller fan in the nose provided pitch control and additional lift. The wing fans rotated in opposite directions and were covered by hinged doors, while the nose fan was covered by louvers. (NASA History Office Collection)

Two XV-5As were manufactured by Ryan. The first (62-4505) flew as a conventional aircraft on 25 May 1964. The first hover was in June 1964 and the first transition in November 1964. Unfortunately, the first airplane crashed in April 1965, killing the pilot. The program had logged 388 flights when the second aircraft (62-4506) crashed in October 1966, also killing the pilot. However, the second airframe was rebuilt for NASA as the XV-5B with a wider landing gear and an improved cockpit. It began flying on 24 June 1968 and was subsequently retired to the Army Aviation Museum at Fort Rucker, Alabama. (NASA Langley Research Center)

Six Hawker FGA.1 Kestrels were brought to the United States for Tri-Service testing under the designation VZ-12, although this was soon changed to XV-6A. Two aircraft were later transferred to NASA. NASA 520 (ex-RAF XS694, ex-USAF 64-18267) was retired to the lawn outside the NASA Langley cafeteria. The aircraft is now in the Virginia Air and Space Center in Hampton, Virginia. (Dave Ostrowski via the Mick Roth Collection)

The Bell XV-3 tilt-rotor began as a joint Army-Air Force program in 1951. The first aircraft made its initial flight as a helicopter in August 1955, but crashed two months later before completing a full conversion. Extensive wind tunnel tests were conducted at NASA Ames, with pilots practicing the conversion process and gear changes (which required significant manipulation of the pitch and throttle controls and took about 20 seconds) in the tunnel. Rotor instability led to the original 23-foot three-bladed full-articulated rotors being replaced by 24-foot two-bladed semi-rigid rotors. The second XV-3 made its first flight on 12 December 1958, with a full conversion only six days later. The XV-3 made 110 full conversions and over 250 flights before it was damaged in a wind tunnel test in 1965 when a rotor housing separated from the aircraft. (NASA Ames Research Center)

The Tri-Service testing of the Kestrels included 374 flights at Edwards AFB. Other tests included an operational demonstration aboard the aircraft carrier USS Independence (CVA-62) and the amphibious landing ship USS Raleigh (LPD-1). The other Kestrel that came to NASA was called NASA 521 (ex-RAF XS689, ex-USAF 64-18263). This aircraft is now at the Virginia Air and Space Center in Hampton, Virginia. (NASA Langley Research Center)

Not truly an X-Plane, the Rockwell XFV-12A still deserves a mention only because it was one of the more interesting projects of the 1970s. Cobbled together from pieces of an A-4 and F-4, Rockwell believed that production FV-12s could take off and land vertically as well as cruise at Mach 2. Here is the only prototype on 30 November 1977 in the Dynamics Research Facility at NASA Langley. The program was cancelled in 1981. (NASA Langley Research Center)

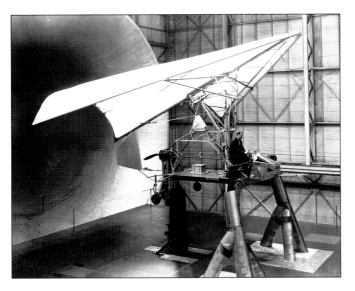

The Ryan XV-8A Fleep (short for "Flying Jeep") was used as a flying research platform for the Rogallo flexible wing. Two aircraft were ordered (USAF serials 63-13003 and 13004), but the second vehicle was never completed. The little ultralight-like aircraft was tested in the NASA Langley 30x60-foot full-scale tunnel during 1962. This is one of the places where the U.S. military designation system falls apart – the AV-8 Harrier duplicating the "V-8") designation originally assigned to the Fleep. (NASA Langley Research Center)

Charles H. Zimmerman with a tilt-wing VTOL model at NASA Langley. ZImmerman moved from Langley to Chance Vought in 1937 but returned to Langley in 1948. Zimmerman was an innovative designer of, among other aircraft, the Vought V-173 and XFSU-1 Flying Pancakes. He developed concepts for flying jeep-like hovercraft, and also heavily influenced the XC-142 V/STOL transport design, which was generally similar to the model above. (NASA Langley Research Center)

The XV-6A was the first model of what became the Harrier attack aircraft and represents one of the few VTOL aircraft to enter operational service. A single turbofan supplies air to four rotating nozzles that can be rotated through 90 degrees, providing a column of air during vertical flight, or to the rear for conventional flight. (left: NASA Langley Research Center; right: John Hathaway via the Mick Roth Collection)

AERODYNAMIC TESTS

Typical of many early jet fighters, engine access in the X-4 was by removing the aft fuselage. Here the two sections are in close proximity on assembly jigs during construction at the Northrop plant in Hawthorne, California. (Northrop via the Gerald H. Balzer Collection)

The first X-4 was initially painted a light grey, but both aircraft spent the majority of the flight program painted an overall white. The small size of the X-4 is well illustrated here with two technicians posing next to it. (Northrop via the Tony Landis Collection)

The first X-4 undergoing a fuel tank check during construction. the aircraft was lifting into a variety of positions to see if the integral wing tanks leaked. Note the special cradle attached the fuselage for lifting. (Northrop via the Gerald H. Balzer Collection)

The Northrop X-4 was the first example of an X-Plane intended to research something besides supersonic flight. The jet-powered X-4 was designed to evaluate the characteristics of a tailless aircraft at high subsonic speeds, a configuration believed to hold a great deal of promise for future aircraft. Although not designed for supersonic speeds, the X-4 nevertheless proved that tailless swept-wing aircraft were not well suited – given available flight-control technology – for high transonic or supersonic performance. Pitch, roll, and yaw insta-bilities were very pronounced at speeds in excess of Mach 0.88, and there was no solution to the problem using the technology available at the time. It is notable that both aircraft survived the flight test program, and there were no serious accidents during 112 flights (the first X-4 only completed 10 of those before being grounded and used as spare parts). The first X-4 is currently on display at Edwards AFB. The second aircraft, after long being displayed at Maxwell AFB, Alabama, is currently at the Air Force Museum at Wright-Patterson AFB, Ohio.

The second X-4 (46-677) also wore a light grey scheme before being repainted white. Given Jack Northrop's long fascination with tailless and flying wing designs, it was natural that his company should build the first tailless X-Plane. (Northrop via the Tony Landis Collection)

At the beginning of the jet age, some aerodynamicists believed that a tailless design might prove significantly less prone to the transonic instability problems that were being suffered by conventional designs. (NASA Dryden Flight Research Center)

The high-visibility red stripes appear to be over the light grey paint on the first X-4, but similar stripes were also associated with the white paint scheme on the second airplane. Given its unique configuration, the airplane flew surprisingly well. (AFFTC History Office Collection)

The first X-4 on a thrust-measuring device at Muroc Air Force Base in October 1949. Several mechanical problems affected the first X-4, and it was quickly grounded and used for parts to keep the second airplane flying. (AFFTC History Office Collection)

This unusual moment-of-inertia test was conducted in the original NACA hangar on South Base on 8 December 1952. The inertias were measured by balancing the vehicle on knife edges supported by calibrated springs. (NASA Dryden Flight Research Center)

The single-piece bubble canopy provided excellent visibility. Note the NACA markings on the vertical stabilizer and upper surface of the far wing. The stripe on the fuselage was a photo reference mark-ing. (NASA Dryden Flight Research Center)

Here are the later Air Force markings on the second X-4 – overall gloss white with a red fin cap. The first X-4 flight was on 16 December 1948, with the last occurring on 29 September 1953. (AFFTC History Office Collection)

An X-4 and D-558-I Skystreak on display at the Antelope Valley Fair on 17 September 1953. Considering that the first X-4 had not flown in over three years, it looks decidedly well cared for, complete with NACA markings. (NASA Dryden Flight Research Center)

The Messerschmitt P.1101 at the Bell plant with an Allison J35 installed. The X-5's resemblance to the Messerschmitt is undeniable. The P.1101 was captured at the Oberammergau, Bavaria, test facility in 1945. The wings of the German aircraft had to be adjusted on the ground before flight. (Jay Miller Collection)

The Bell X-5 was the first variable-geometry aircraft to fly, and was largely based on the design of the German Messerschmitt P.1101 that was captured near the end of World War II and brought to the United States for technical review and inspection. After spending three years at Wright Field, the aircraft was turned over to Bell Aircraft, which had already been studying variable-geometry versions of the X-1 design in the wind tunnel at Langley. The P.1101 seemed to offer an expedient way to gain early flight experience with a swing-wing airplane. Unfortunately, the P.1101 was damaged while being delivered to Bell, and in any event, the company was unable to decide on an engine to use in the relatively small airframe. Instead, Bell proposed building 24 interceptor versions of a larger swing-wing aircraft for operational evaluation. The Air Force was interested and initiated Project MX-1095, which ultimately resulted in the construction of two X-5s that differed from their German ancestor primarily in being able to adjust their wing sweep angle in flight. The angle of the variable sweep wing could be adjusted from 20 to 60 degrees, and the X-5 provided a great deal of data for programs such as the Grumman XF10F-1 and General Dynamics F-111. The single surviving X-5 was retired from service in 1955, and is now on display at the Air Force Museum at Wright-Patterson AFB, Ohio.

The first X-5 (50-1838) at the Bell plant. Note the X-5 logo on the nose and compare it to the photo at right. This X-5 would make its first flight on 20 June 1951 at Edwards AFB and is currently displayed at the Air Force Museum. (Jay Miller Collection)

The first X-5 taxis in after a test flight at Edwards. Note the stylized logo on the nose and the addition of the AFFTC badge. The X-5 logo changed several times on the first airplane, and it appears the second airplane never carried it. (AFFTC History Office Collection)

Composite photo showing the range of motion of the wing on the X-5. Unlike later design where the pivot point was fixed, on the X-5 the pivot point moved forward as the wings swept aft to maintain the center of pressure and center-of-gravity. (AFFTC History Office Collection)

The first X-5 lands after its second flight on 25 June 1951. A T-33 and F-80 were acting as chase aircraft. Note the X-5 logo is missing from the nose. A number of notable test pilots eventually flew the X-5, including Neil Armstrong, Albert Boyd, Scott Crossfield, Frank Everest, John McKay, and Joe Walker. (AFFTC History Office Collection)

This 4 January 1952 view of X-5 shows the flaps down and speed brakes extended. The speedbrakes proved to be poorly located and were seldom used in flight since they caused a severe buffeting when deployed. (NASA Dryden Flight Research Center)

The P.1101 heritage was obvious from almost any angle. Note the segmented main landing gear doors and the small ventral stabilizer. At various times Bell proposed substituting a Westinghouse J46 for the J35, but this never occurred. (Museum of Flight via Jay Miller)

The first X-5 in flight over Edwards North Base. The wide flight envelope of the X-5 – from 150 mph to 550 mph – made it an ideal chase plane, and it was occasionally used for that purpose. (AFFTC History Office Collection)

The spin characteristics of the X-5 were not particularly good, and the second X-5 was lost in a flat spin on 14 October 1953. This crash claimed the life of Major Raymond Popson. Note the original Flight Test Center logo on the fuselage. (AFFTC History Office Collection)

The X-5 used a conventional tricycle retractable landing gear, with all three units being hydraulically retracted rearward into the fuselage. Sometimes, however, things just do not work as planned. This is the first X-5 after the left main landing gear failed while touching down on 26 March 1953 after its 71st flight. NASA test pilot Joe Walker was not injured. (NASA Dryden Flight Research Center)

The Northrop X-21A Laminar Flow Control testbed was designed to explore the feasibility of using full-scale boundary layer control on a large aircraft. Analytical and wind tunnel studies conducted by Northrop had indicated boundary layer control would offer numerous performance benefits. After successfully demonstrating the ability to achieve laminar flow over approximately 75 percent of the wing surface, the X-21As were used to explore the impact of rain, sleet, snow, and other weather anomalies on the system. During the flight test program, the X-21As demonstrated that the boundary layer control technique, called laminar flow control, was both effective and viable. However, they also showed that these benefits came with a significant maintenance penalty – the numerous small slots required for the airflow constantly plugged up. The two X-21As were converted from Douglas WB-66D light bombers that had been retired from active service. Both X-21As survived the flight test program and are currently in a bad state of repair on the photo range at Edwards AFB.

Other than the basic fuselage shell, there was not much remaining of the WB-66Ds by the time Northrop had finished modifying them. The wing was new, and the center and aft fuselages were extensively strengthened. (AFFTC History Office Collection)

The second X-21A (55-0410) is towed from the hangar at the NASA Flight Research Center on 20 October 1966. This airplane never received the white paint worn by the first airplane, and the original Air Force markings can still be seen on the natural metal surfaces. The large pods under the wings contained the pumping units for the laminar flow control system. (NASA Dryden Flight Research Center)

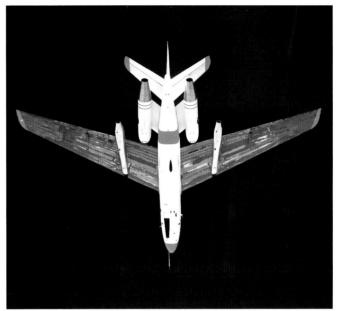

The first X-21A (55-0408) over Edwards AFB. Originally, the second WB-66D to be converted into an X-21A was supposed to be 55-0409, but a landing accident on the delivery flight to Northrop damaged the aircraft beyond economical repair. A third aircraft, 55-0410, was selected as a replacement. (Northrop via Tony Chong)

The theory was that boundary-layer air could be sucked from the surface of the wing, improving the laminar flow characteristics of the wing. There were 16,986 linear feet of suction slots that varied in width from 0.003- to 0.010-inch on the X-21 wing. The pumps in the pods sucked air through the slots. (AFFTC History Office Collection)

Both X-21As survived the test program, and were stripped of all useable parts and placed on the photo range at Edwards. The first airplane is in the left photo, taken on 16 July 1997, while the second airplane is shown at right on the same date. The geometric patterns nearby are photo calibration targets. (NASA Dryden Flight Research Center Collection)

The concept of the forward swept wing had been tested during World War II, but when these early tests were conducted, strong lightweight materials were not readily available. Models of the X-1 were also tested with forward-swept wings, but it was not until the late 1970s and 1980s that new materials allowed reasonable testing to begin. Unfortunately, the perceived drag reductions were not realized. Two Grumman X-29As served as testbeds for aerodynamics, composite building techniques, and advanced avionics. Although most X-29A flights were conducted from Edwards AFB, one X-29A was flown to the Dayton (Ohio) International Air Show and to the Experimental Aircraft Association (EAA) International Convention and Sport Aviation Exhibition at Oshkosh, Wisconsin. The first X-29 was retired to the Air Force Museum, and the second aircraft is on display at the Dryden Flight Research Center. The National Air and Space Museum has a full-scale X-29 mockup on display.

General Dynamics proposed modifying the basic F-16 with a forward-swept wing. (General Dynamics via the Tony Landis Collection)

During the mid-1970s Rockwell pitched a forward-swept wing design called the Sabre Bat. DARPA used this basic design as a basis for the X-29. (Rockwell International via the Tony Landis Collection)

The first X-29 was moved from Port Jefferson to Bayonne, New York, by barge, then by container ship to San Pedro, California. It arrived at Edwards on a flatbed trailer. (NASA Dryden Flight Research Center)

In-flight refueling tests were conducted during June 1988 with the first X-29 (83-0003) behind the NKC-135 assigned to Edwards. Since the X-29 did not have a refueling receptacle, the tests did not involve actual hookups but proved that the X-29 did not exhibit any undesirable behavior when flying in close proximity to the tanker. (left: NASA Dryden Flight Research Center; right: AFFTC History Office Collection)

The second X-29 (82-0049) was delivered to Edwards on 6 November 1988, following much the same route taken by the first airplane. (NASA Dryden Flight Research Center)

The second airplane made its first flight on 23 May 1989, with an AFFTC T-38 acting as chase. Note the spin chute container behind the X-29 vertical stabilizer. (NASA Dryden Flight Research Center)

The second X-29 was fitted with a set of cardboard dummy missiles on 8 February 1991, but it was never flown in this configuration. The F-5A forward fuselage used to lower costs is clearly evident here. (NASA Dryden Flight Research Center)

South Base and Rogers Dry Lake as seen by a wing-mounted camera on the second X-29 on 24 September 1991. A smoke generator was installed in the aircraft nose to show airflow patterns at high angles of attack. (NASA Dryden Flight Research Center)

The X-29s used a single General Electric F404-GE-400 powerplant from the F/A-18A. (NASA Dryden Flight Research Center)

X-Planes Photo Scrapbook

Both X-29s pose together on 16 November 1990, with the first aircraft on the left. Note the stripe on the vertical stabilizer – left side only – of the second aircraft. (NASA Dryden Flight Research Center)

In addition to the canards and rudder, there were leading edge surfaces on each wing, four trailing edge flaps on the wings, and two more flaps at the rear of the trailing edge strakes. This is the first aircraft on 20 December 1985. (NASA Dryden Flight Research Center)

A spin chute was added to the second aircraft as a safety precaution for the high angle-of-attack trials during mid-1989. The last X-29 flight was in October 1991 at the AFFTC Open House at Edwards. (NASA Dryden Flight Research Center)

The Rockwell X-31 Enhanced Fighter Maneuverability (EFM) demonstrator provided information for the designs of the next generation of highly maneuverable fighters. The X-31 demonstrated in-flight thrust vectoring coupled with advanced flight control systems at very high angles of attack. The result was a significant advantage over most conventional fighters in close-in-combat situations. Three thrust vectoring paddles made of graphite epoxy and mounted on the aft fuselage were directed into the engine exhaust plume to provide control in pitch and yaw. In addition, the X-31 was configured with movable forward canards, wing control surfaces, and fixed aft strakes. During the program's initial phase of flight test operations at the Rockwell Aerospace facility in Palmdale, California, the two aircraft were flown on 108 test missions, performing in-flight thrust vectoring and expanding the post-stall envelope to 40 degrees angle of attack. Operations were then moved to nearby Edwards AFB in February 1992. At Dryden, the International Test Organization (ITO) expanded the aircraft's flight envelope, including military utility evaluations that pitted the X-31 against modern fighter aircraft to evaluate the maneuverability of the X-31 in simulated combat. The first X-31 was lost on 19 January 1995 – the pilot, Karl Lang, ejected safely at 18,000 feet before the aircraft crashed. The second X-31 completed the 580th and last flight of its original research program on 13 May 1995 and was placed in storage. The aircraft was subsequently shipped to NAS Patuxent River in April 2000, where it was largely rebuilt for the VECTOR (Vectoring Extremely Short Take-Off and Landing Control Tailless Operation Research) program. The revised aircraft made its first flight on 24 February 2001. After two months of basic flight testing, the aircraft began a year of upgrading and ground testing in preparation for demonstrating extremely short takeoff and landing (ESTOL) landings to a "virtual runway" at 5,000 feet altitude. The X-31 took to the air again on 17 May 2002. In its final flight on 29 April 2003, the X-31 performed the last in a series of fully automated ESTOL landings on an actual runway, approaching at a high 24-degree angle of attack (twice the normal 12-degree AOA) at only 121 knots (more than 30 percent slower than the normal 175 knot landing speed). The aircraft is currently in storage at Pax River.

The second X-31 (BuNo 164585) during high angle-of-attack testing at Edwards on 15 March 1994. Note the three thrust-vectoring paddle behind the engine exhaust. (NASA Dryden photo by Jim Ross)

The first X-31 (164584) preparing for its first flight at Palmdale on 11 October 1990. The X-31 was powered by a single General Electric F404-GE-400. (Rockwell International via the Tony Landis Collection)

The U.S. government and Rockwell wanted to display the X-31 at the Paris air show in 1995, and also perform demonstration flights in Europe. However, an analysis showed that the shorter runways available in Germany and France would necessitate the addition of a drag chute. This is the first deployment of the drag chute on 12 May 1995 during a test at Edwards. (NASA Dryden Flight Research Center)

The first X-31 participated in carrier landing trials on the runway at North Base during December 1995. This was the last time ship one was photographed before being lost on 19 January 1995 during the 524th flight of the program. (NASA Dryden Flight Research Center)

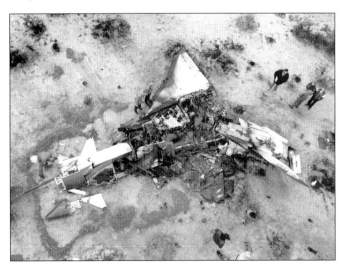

The crash site on the day after the accident. The pitot system had unknowingly iced, resulting in a loss of control. Test pilot Karl-Heinz Lang from Germany successfully ejected, but the aircraft – obviously – was a complete loss. (NASA Dryden Flight Research Center)

The surviving X-31A returns to Pax River after a VECTOR test flight on 14 November 2002. The German and American flags were prominently displayed on the vertical stabilizer, and the Navy frequently referred to VECTOR as the "first international X-Plane," although this seemingly ignored the XV-6 Kestrel and several others from the 1960s. (U.S. Marine Corps photo by Maj. Cody Allee)

For a period during 1994-95, some limited funding for the X-31 came from the JAST (Joint Advanced Strike Technology) program that later evolved into the Joint Strike Fighter (JSF). Note the JAST logo on the nose. (NASA Dryden Flight Research Center)

This photo from 31 May 1995 shows the second X-31 at Edwards along with all ground support equipment necessary for flying a mission. This also gives a good sense of how small the X-31 was. (NASA Dryden photo by Jim Ross)

Both X-31s together on the ramp at Palmdale on 22 June 1991. The aircraft would go on to fly more missions than any other X-Plane, numbering nearly 600 by the time the VECTOR program was completed in 2002. (Rockwell International via the Tony Landis Collection)

The X-31 takes off from NAS Patuxent River, Maryland, on a VECTOR test flight on 17 May 2002. (U.S. Navy photo by James Darcy)

Three thrust-vectoring aircraft fly in formation on 15 March 1994: the NASA 840 F/A-18A High Alpha Research Vehicle (HARV), the second X-31, and the Variable Stability In-Flight Simulator Test Aircraft (VISTA) NF-16D. The only one missing is the Advanced Control Technology for Integrated Vehicles (ACTIVE) NF-15B. Interestingly, none of the technologies demonstrated in these aircraft have made it to production. (NASA Dryden Flight Research Center)

THE LIFTING BODIES

NASA test pilot Milt Thompson sits in the mockup of the M2-F1 on 8 November 1962. The flat-top and round-bottom shape of the lifting body show up well here. (NASA Dryden Flight Research Center)

Five months later, on 4 April 1963, Milt Thompson sat in the real M2-F1. The lifting body was originally fitted with a large center stabilizer, but never flew with it. (NASA Dryden Flight Research Center)

Two of the more unique air vehicles to be tested at the Flight Research Center during the 1960s. The M2-F1 lifting body and Paresev pose together on 5 November 1963. (NASA Dryden Flight Research Center)

This was underneath the plywood shape of the M2-F1. Note the bungee cords used as shock absorbers on the Cessna 150 main gear. Originally, plans included flying several different body shapes using the same internal structure. (NASA Dryden Flight Research Center)

The lifting body program involved several different vehicles – the M2, HL-10, X-23A, and X-24 – that provided data on wingless lifting bodies from orbital reentry velocities to approach and landing speeds. The manned lifting body program began in September 1962 when R. Dale Reed at the NASA Flight Research Center began work on the M2-F1. This plywood vehicle was towed behind various trucks and cars to get airborne, and proved the basic concept. NASA then awarded a contract to Northrop to build a metal version called the M2-F2, powered by a Reaction Motors XLR11 rocket engine left over from the X-15 program. After a serious crash on 10 May 1967, the airframe was rebuilt as the M2-F3 with a central vertical stabilizer that largely cured an earlier stability problem. The HL-10 was a totally different shape, but shared many common systems with the M2-F2/3 and was also powered by an XLR11. Its first flight was on 22 December 1966, and the HL-10 would ultimately become the fastest and highest flying of the manned lifting bodies. The X-23 was an unmanned version of the basic X-24 shape that was launched on Atlas boosters and verified that lifting bodies could return from orbit. Like the M2-F2/3 and HL-10, the X-24 was used for supersonic and landing evaluations of the shape. For more on the lifting body story, pick up a copy of Dale Reed (with Darlene Lister), Wingless Flight, NASA SP-4220, available from the Government Printing Office or the NASA History Office.

Milt Thompson checking out a trio of future M2 pilots – Chuck Yeager, Don Mallick, and Bruce Peterson – on 16 September 1963. The canopy on the M2-F1 lifted off instead of being hinged. The entire vehicle was built locally in a matter of a few months using volunteer labor and a few small contracts. (NASA Dryden Flight Research Center)

The little plywood M2-F1 being towed by the NASA R4D (otherwise known as a DC-3 or C-47) on 28 February 1964. Note the small elevons – these would not make the transition to the metal M2-F2. (NASA Dryden Flight Research Center)

Originally the M2-F1 was towed behind a NASA pickup truck. When higher-speed tows became necessary, this Pontiac convertible was procured. Note the passenger seat faces backwards and the side-facing back seats. (NASA Dryden Flight Research Center)

Late in its flight program, the M2-F1 was fitted with a small solid rocket engine to help the vehicle flare during landing (a sign near the engine read "Instant L/D"). The aircraft carried an "N" number on the rudders. Note the configuration of the windows in the nose and forward fuselage to provide downward visibility during landing. (AFFTC History Office Collection)

The M2-F1 was only 20 feet long and 14 feet wide. It weighed just over 1,100 pounds, although this was almost double the 600 pounds Dale Reed had originally estimated. Total cost of the glider was about $30,000. (NASA Dryden Flight Research Center)

The plywood M2-F1 glider poses next to the all-metal, rocket-powered M2-F2 on 14 February 1966. The basic shape had been refined considerably through wind tunnel testing and the limited glide experience of the M2-F1. (NASA Dryden Flight Research Center)

The all-metal M2-F2 in the full-scale wind tunnel at the NASA Ames Research Center on 27 August 1965. (NASA Ames Research Center)

The M2-F2 at the rollout on 15 June 1965 at Northrop's Hawthorne plant. (Northrop via the Tony Landis Collection)

Jerry Gentry lands the M2-F2 after Flight M-14-21 on 21 November 1966. Gentry was once quoted as saying, "There was no question which way you were going when the B-52 dropped you ... one guy used to say that if they dropped a brick out of the B-52 at the same time, he'd beat the brick to the ground." Note the colorful F-104N chase plane. (NASA Dryden Flight Research Center)

The venerable NB-52A carried the M2-F2 on a special adapter attached to the X-15 pylon under the wing. This is Flight M-5-12 on 2 September 1966. (AFFTC History Office Collection)

As part of the M2-F2 contract, Northrop manufactured the adapters that mated the lifting body with the X-15 pylon under the right wing of the two NB-52 carrier aircraft. Here is the M2-F2 attached to the *NB-52A on 23 September 1965.* (AFFTC History Office Collection)

The M2-F2 and HL-10 were special cases in which NASA contracted to have a vehicle manufactured instead of using an aircraft procured by one of the military services. *Here is the M2-F2 on 24 February 1966.* (AFFTC History Office Collection)

The lifting-body was thought to offer advantages for the soon-to-be Space Shuttle, and there were proposals to fly a space-rated M2 shape into orbit and return to verify its very-high-speed characteristics, much like was done with the X-23A. However, interest waned before this happened. (NASA Dryden Flight Research Center)

Bruce Peterson had a very bad day during Flight M-16-24 on 10 May 1967, the last planned glide flight before powered flight test began. The M2-F2 was nearly uncontrollable and tumbled end-over-end during landing, a sequence played at the beginning of every episode of the Six Million Dollar Man television show. Peterson was seriously injured and lost the use of one eye, but otherwise recovered from the accident. Earlier in the year the lifting body had been modified to carry its XLR11 engine (compare the shape of the body flap in the left photo with the photo on the facing page, and note the vent tubes for the propellants), but the engine was not installed on this flight (the engine bay has a cover over it) and the M2-F2 never made a powered flight. Note Peterson's helmet on the ground in the photo at right. (NASA Dryden Flight Research Center)

The M2-F2 airframe was rebuildable, and the solution was to add the large center stabilizer that had originally been fitted to the M2-F1. During the rebuilding, it was announced that Bill Dana would be the new project pilot, so the crews put a special tailband on the aircraft to mark the occasion. The photo is dated 22 July 1969. (NASA Dryden Flight Research Center)

In addition to the new center stabilizer, the aft fuselage was made deeper to accommodate the XLR11 engine without having to modify the body flap. Compare the body flap with the photo at above left and also on the facing page. Bill Dana would take the M2-F3 for its first glide flight on 2 June 1970 and found that its handling qualities were much improved. (NASA Dryden Flight Research Center)

The M2-F3 venting during an engine test. The XLR11s used by the lifting bodies were surplus engines from the X-15 program that had been rescued from various museums. (Bill Dana Collection)

The slightly deeper aft-fuselage of the M2-F3 allowed a much cleaner XLR11 engine installation than had been possible with the original M2-F2. Each of the four chambers of the XLR11 could be lit and extinguished independently. (AFFTC History Office Collection)

This artwork by NASA engineer Wen Painter poked fun at the recovery techniques used by the on-going Gemini program. Note the seasick astronauts in the capsule and the red carpet at the Los Angeles airport for the M2. (NASA Dryden Flight Research Center)

Another difference the M2-F2 and M2-F3 was the window in the nose. On the M2-F2 this had been a single piece of wraparound plexiglass. As can be seen here, on the M2-F3 it was two pieces with a wide center support. (NASA Dryden Flight Research Center)

The fixed-base lifting body simulator at the NASA Flight Research Center. Note the large plotting board just behind the cockpit. (NASA Dryden Flight Research Center)

The cockpit of the M2 was simple. Toggle switches to ignite each chamber of the XLR11 are on the left side console. (NASA Dryden Flight Research Center)

The chase planes were always close by, sometimes very close, as this photo shows. Although a variety of aircraft were used as chase, the Air Force used T-38s more often than not, while NASA used its *F-104N Starfighters.* (AFFTC History Office Collection)

The M2-F3 venting just before release. This perspective gives a good idea how far forward the lifting body was mounted under the wing of the NB-52. The M2 made 43 flights – 16 as the M2-F2 and 27 as the rebuilt M2-F3. (AFFTC History Office Collection)

When the Flight Research Center solicited bids to build the mission-weight M2 and HL-10 gliders, only five companies submitted proposals. Most of the contractors estimated it would cost $15 million for the two vehicles, substantially more than NASA had available. Northrop thought it could do it for about $2.5 million, assuming NASA would allow the company considerable freedom and not overly burden them with documentation. The two vehicles were delivered on time and for slightly less than the estimate. (AFFTC History Office Collection)

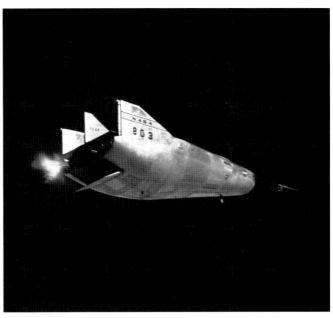

The M2-F3 launches from the NB-52. Note the position of the body flap during launch. The XLR11 rocket engine produced enough thrust to power the 5,000-pound lifting body to a maximum of Mach 1.613 during a flight on 13 December 1972. (AFFTC History Office Collection)

By the end of the lifting body program, the NASA F-104Ns had given up their colorful markings for the better-known blue and white paint scheme. This photo shows just how small the M2-F3 was compared to the Starfighter. (AFFTC History Office Collection)

On 20 December 1972 John Manke took the M2-F3 to 71,493 feet during the highest, and last, flight of the program. The flight had reached Mach 1.294 and had tested an experimental reaction control system. (AFFTC History Office Collection)

The HL-10 during Flight H-26-40 on 30 September 1969. Note the unusual chase aircraft – a Douglas F5D-1 Skylancer. The Skylancer had been used by the Flight Research Center for Dyna-Soar simulations, and was occasionally flown as chase. (AFFTC History Office Collection)

This 28-foot-long model (6 feet longer than the actual vehicle) of the HL-10 was tested in the 30x60-foot full-scale wind tunnel at NASA Langley in 1964. Several different configurations were evaluated, with this being the one ultimately built. (NASA Langley Research Center)

The HL-10 under the wing of the NB-52B on 15 December 1966. The HL-10 was carried on the same NB-52 carrier aircraft pylon adapter as the M2-F2. The first HL-10 glide flight took place a week after this photo, on 22 December 1966. (NASA Dryden Flight Research Center)

The HL-10 (Horizontal Lander, model number 10) shape was developed at NASA Langley based on studies that had begun as early as 1957. The white paint was added to cover the new fiberglass leading edges on the tip fins. (NASA Dryden Flight Research Center)

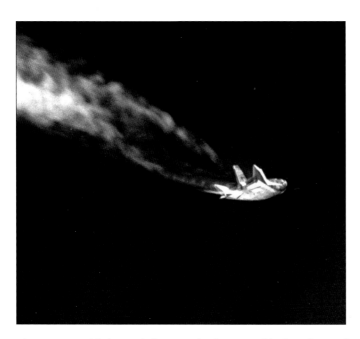

The HL-10 would ultimately become the fastest and highest flying of the lifting bodies, reaching Mach 1.86 on 18 February 1970 and 90,303 feet nine days later. (NASA Dryden Flight Research Center)

Like the M2-F2 and X-24, the HL-10 used a single Reaction Motors XLR11 rocket engine. This was the same type of engine used in the X-1, D-558-II, and early X-15s. (NASA Dryden Flight Research Center)

Boys will be boys, and these four continued a tradition begun with the X-15 pilots a decade earlier. The HL-10 pilots – Jerry Gentry, Pete Hoag, John Manke, and Bill Dana – posed for their official portrait (left) and unofficial rumpus on 17 June 1970. (NASA Dryden Flight Research Center)

Several cone and half-cone shapes were tested in the NASA Langley 30x60 tunnel prior to the HL-10 design being finalized. This particular test is from 1959. (NASA Langley Research Center)

A model of the final HL-10 configuration in the NASA Langley spin Tunnel during 1964. This facility allows researchers to investigate the spin characteristics of a design. (NASA Langley Research Center)

An early model of the HL-10 in the NASA Langley 30x60-foot full scale wind tunnel in 1964. Note that there is only a central dorsal stabilizer, and that the upswept tip fins have not been added yet. (NASA Langley Research Center)

As finally built, the HL-10 had three vertical surfaces, much like the modified M2-F3. The tip fins were extensions of the bottom and sides of the fuselage, while a tall central dorsal stabilizer was between the upper body flaps. (NASA Dryden Flight Research Center)

Like the M2-F2, the HL-10 was built by Northrop in Hawthorne, and was rolled out on 18 January 1966. It was shipped to Edwards for installation of various systems, then delivered to the NASA Ames Research Center for additional wind tunnel testing. Here it is at Edwards on 30 April 1966. (NASA Dryden Flight Research Center)

The wind tunnel testing at Ames revealed minor flow separation around the tip fins, but it was not believed to be serious. Bruce Peterson proved otherwise on the first glide flight, when he barely managed to land intact. It took 15 months for engineers to resolve the problem. (NASA Dryden Flight Research Center)

After additional wind tunnel tests at NASA Ames, it was decided to modify the leading edge of the tip fins to direct more airflow over the control surfaces. This seemingly minor change corrected the stability problem. (NASA Dryden Flight Research Center)

The HL-10 under the wing of the NB-52B. Note the lifting body mission marks on the carrier aircraft. The blister on the B-52 fuselage housed a camera that allowed the launch operator to observe the research airplane. (NASA Dryden Flight Research Center)

The Air Force also had a lifting body program, designated X-24A. These used the SV-5 shape developed by Martin Marietta and were essentially larger-scale versions of the X-23A PRIME vehicle that made several suborbital reentry tests during 1966 and 1967. (AFFTC History Office Collection)

While the X-23A had demonstrated that the Martin shape was stable in very high-speed flight and reentry, the Air Force wanted to verify that the shape was controllable at supersonic, transonic, and landing speeds. Like all of the lifting bodies, the X-24A spent a lot of time in wind tunnels. (NASA Dryden Flight Research Center)

The X-24A, shown on 15 July 1971, used the same XLR11 rocket engine as the NASA lifting bodies, although the installation was not as clean as the Northrop vehicles. The X-24A weighed about 6,000 pounds empty, increasing to 11,000 pounds fully loaded with a pilot and propellants. (NASA Dryden Flight Research Center)

The X-24A, like the HL-10, used two sets of split flaps – top and bottom – for pitch control; the M2 used split upper flaps and a single lower flap. Two segment rudders were located on each tip fin. Note the empty rocket motor mounting location and the propellant vent tubes. (NASA Dryden Flight Research Center)

This photo of an unpainted X-24A shows the flat bottom and half-round top and how the tip fins are a continuation of the gentle bottom curve. The vehicle would be coated with a rough ablator prior to being tested in a wind tunnel at the NASA Ames Research Center. (NASA Dryden Flight Research Center)

Although all three lifting bodies ultimately used three verticals, the control surfaces differed considerably. The X-24A used two segment rudders on each tip fin; the HL-10 used spilt rudders on all three surfaces; and the M2-F3 used outboard rudders on the tip fins only. (NASA Dryden Flight Research Center)

The two NB-52s got quite a workout in the 1960s and early 1970s between the X-15 and the three lifting body programs. After lugging around the 50,000-pound X-15A-2, the 10,000-pound lifting bodies seemed light. (NASA Dryden Flight Research Center)

X-Planes Photo Scrapbook

The X-24A was shipped to NASA Ames – a few hundred miles away near San Jose – twice, and each time by truck. The outer fuselage sides and tip fins were removed for transit, allowing a good look at the main landing gear. (NASA Dryden Flight Research Center)

When the X-24A flight program ended on 4 June 1971, a decision was made to modify the vehicle into the X-24B. It was partially disassembled and loaded into a C-130 to the trip back to the Martin plant in Maryland on 17 December. (NASA Dryden Flight Research Center)

Martin also proposed building a trio of jet-powered lifting bodies called the SV-5J for pilot training. The vehicles used a single 3,000-lbf Pratt & Whitney J60 jet engine, were considered very underpowered, and they never flew. (NASA Dryden Flight Research Center)

An SV-5 (X-23/24) shape mounted on the nose of a booster. This is just a traveling exhibit parked at the Air Force Academy, but gives a good indication of the Air Force's intentions concerning manned space flight. (U.S. Air Force via the Tony Landis Collection)

X-Planes Photo Scrapbook

The X-24A undergoes a mating test with the NB-52A on 20 October 1967. After this it was transported via truck to NASA Ames for additional wind tunnel tests, then returned to Edwards in time for the first glide flight on 17 April 1968. (NASA Dryden Flight Research Center)

An X-24A engine run in 1968. Initially the NASA rocket engine shop built and maintained the XLR11s for the lifting bodies since the Air Force rocket engine shop (which normally maintained all of the engines at Edwards) was busy with the XLR99 for the X-15. Eventually, as things wound down, the Air Force took over most maintenance. (NASA Dryden Flight Research Center)

The X-24A was modified with an outer shell based on the FDL-7 shape developed by the Flight Dynamics Laboratory. The new shape was literally bolted on top of the original X-24A. This is the first captive flight of the modified vehicle on 19 July 1973. (AFFTC History Office Collection)

If you stare enough you can see the canopy, humpback, and the three vertical stabilizers of the original X-24A poking out through the sleek FDL-7 body. Originally, the plan had been to use one of the SV-5J pilot trainers, but converting the X-2$A was less expensive since it was already fully functional. (NASA Dryden Flight Research Center)

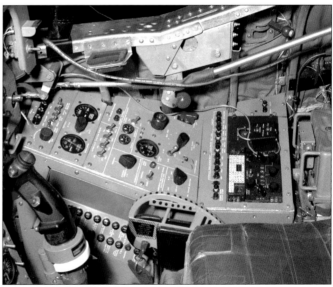

Above and facing page: *The cockpit of the X-24B was conventional, although perhaps a bit more sophisticated than the two Northrop lifting bodies. The XLR11 was controlled via a normal-looking throttle on the left console.* (NASA Dryden Flight Research Center)

X-Planes Photo Scrapbook

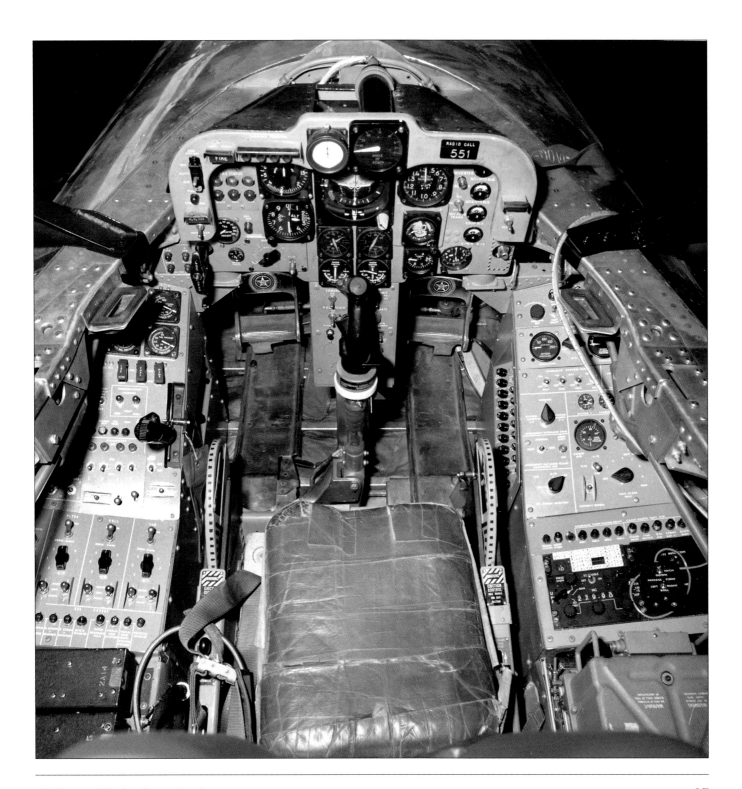

Initially the X-24B forebody was natural metal, while the little that remained of the original X-24A was painted white. Later the entire back two-thirds of the lifting body were painted white, and eventually the vehicle received an overall white scheme with a blue edge and gold trim. (NASA Dryden Flight Research Center)

The X-24B a few seconds after being dropped from the NB-52. Since there are no propellant vapors from the X-24B, this is most likely the first glide flight on 1 August 1973. The first powered flight would follow on 15 November 1973. John Manke flew both missions. (NASA Dryden Flight Research Center)

The new triangular-shaped fuselage presented some problems getting into and out of the cockpit, but nothing that a longer ladder would not solve. All three lifting body programs were accomplished very inexpensively, and little unique support equipment was purchased. (NASA Dryden Flight Research Center)

The X-24B in its final paint scheme, with a NASA F-104 flying chase. Between main landing gear touchdown and nose gear touchdown, the X-24B tended to roll and yaw sharply in the downwind direction. After the vehicle stabilized on all three wheels, the nose wheel steering was adequate. (NASA Dryden Flight Research Center)

X-Planes Photo Scrapbook

A group photo showing the X-24B, NB-52B, three F-104s, a UH-1 res-cue helicopter, some of the ground vehicles, and most of the people involved in the program. (NASA Dryden Flight Research Center)

Not the best quality picture, but the photographer was likely hold-ing on for his life. This illustrates the steep profile flown by the X-24B, with the ever-present F-104 right behind it (with its landing gear out for more drag). (NASA Dryden Flight Research Center)

Bill Dana after the last powered flight of X-24B on 23 September 1973. This was the last rocket-powered research flight at Edwards. Dana had also been the last man to fly the X-15. It had been an exciting 26 years in the desert. (NASA Dryden Flight Research Center)

A posed publicity shot showing the three lifting bodies – the X-24A, M2-F3, and HL-10. (NASA Dryden Flight Research Center)

A different angle of the same lineup of lifting bodies. The X-24A is in the foreground, followed by the M2-F3 and HL-10. (NASA Dryden Flight Research Center)

All of the lifting bodies on display in the NASA hangar. The M2-F3 is in the background, the X-24A is in the middle, and the nose of HL-10 is at right. (NASA Dryden Flight Research Center)

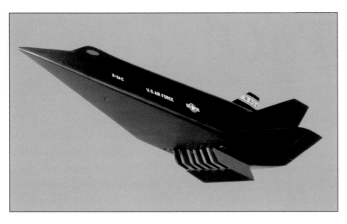

Above: *Several X-24B-derived follow-ons were proposed to continue research in support of the Space Shuttle, much as the X-15 had supported Apollo. Collectively, these are now called X-24Cs, although at the time they had names such as the Hypersonic Facilities Aircraft (HYFAC), Incremental Growth Vehicle (IGV), and National Hypersonic Flight Research Facility (NHFRF – pronounced "nerf"). Most of these were intended to explore flight between Mach 8 and Mach 12, but the $500 million price tag fairly much assured that none would be built. A more austere Hypersonic Technology Integration Demonstrator (HYTID) fared no better.* (Tony Landis Collection)

Above and two below: *In 1969 the Flight Research Center built several radio-controlled models of the NASA Langley Hyper III configuration, a slender re-entry shape with a flat bottom and sides. The Hyper III had a lift-to-drag ratio of about 3, and was designed with a fixed-wing simulating a pop-out wing concept that could be used to increase the low-speed glide ratio of an actual reentry vehicle. The larger Hyper III was built for about $6,500, with the smaller models costing considerably less. The vehicle weighed 485 pounds, was 32 feet long, and spanned 18 feet. The Hyper III was launched from a helicopter at 10,000 feet on 12 December 1969. The vehicle glided 3 miles, reversed course, then glided another 3 miles to its only landing. Although the Hyper III configuration appeared to work, the program was cancelled since the aircraft had a much lower lift-to-drag ratio than predicted.* (NASA Dryden Flight Research Center)

INTO SPACE

This is the Model 814-1050 from March 1959. A team of Boeing and Vought built this full-scale mockup of the Dyna-Soar and its Atlas booster as part of a hard-won battle against a competing team of Martin Marietta and Bell. The X-20 would evolve considerably over the next several years. (Boeing Historical Archives)

One of the most famous X-Planes to never have been built, the Boeing X-20 Dyna-Soar was the final outgrowth of concepts that had begun with Eugen Sänger in 1928 and progressed through the Bell BoMi and RoBo concepts of the 1950s. At some points during its development, the Dyna-Soar was intended to be a quasi-operational system – satellite interceptor, orbital bomber, resupply vehicle. Initially, the Dyna-Soar would be launched on an Atlas booster, although later versions were heavy enough to require a Titan, Titan III, Titan IIIC, and finally a Saturn I. Although the X-20 never progressed beyond the preliminary construction stage, it effectively served as a testbed for a variety of advanced technologies that contributed enormously to various follow-on projects, including the Space Shuttle. In addition, several subsystems developed for the X-20 found their way into the X-15. The X-20 program was cancelled before the first vehicle was completed and most of the subsystems manufactured for the uncompleted vehicle were used for various ground tests. Very few vehicles have contributed more to the science of very high-speed flight – especially vehicles that were never actually built.

A sub-scale model of the X-20 in the 30x60-foot wind tunnel at NASA Langley during 1960. (NASA Langley Research Center)

The cockpit from the 1959 mockup. Compare this to the later version on the following page. (Boeing Historical Archives)

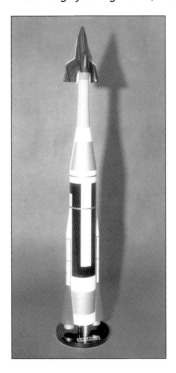
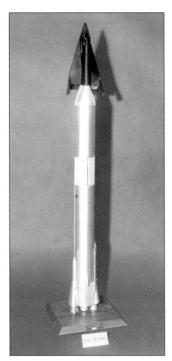
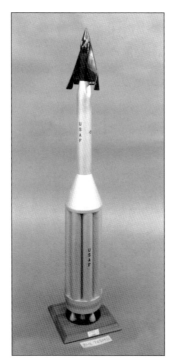
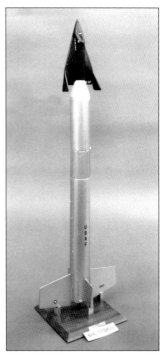

Dyna-Soar models on top of a variety of boosters (from left): Atlas, Atlas-Centaur, Juno 5, and Titan-Centaur. (Boeing Historical Archives)

What is believed to be the final X-20 cockpit layout. Note the three large windows instead of the earlier single small windscreen, and the addition of vertical tape-style instruments. The moving map display in the center of the instrument panel is also much smaller. (Dennis R. Jenkins Collection)

The X-20 was to be the first reusable spacecraft, and a great deal of research was conducted on thermal protection systems. Boeing's teammate, Vought, was at the forefront of this research and went on to develop and build the nose cap and wing leading edges on the *Space Shuttle Orbiter.* (NASA Dryden Flight Research Center)

The first F-100F (56-3725) was modified by the Air Force Systems Command's Aeronautical Systems Division for testing steep approaches and fast landing speeds in support of the X-15 and X-20 programs. In order to perform these tests, means had to be found to provide a large additional drag that could be added or removed on command. To this end, the drag chute and afterburner were replaced by a thrust reverser that could be operated in flight. In addition, the standard belly speedbrake was replaced by a special perforated air brake with almost three times the area. The use of these features enabled the F-100F to touch down at 230 mph rather than the usual 155 mph. (left: AFFTC History Office Collection; right: Terry Panopalis Collection)

The full-scale X-20 mockup was displayed at the Air Force Association convention in Las Vegas in 1962 and represented the final configuration when the program was cancelled. The lower photo at right is unusual in that it shows the windows without the heat shield that was normally in place. (above: Terry Panopalis Collection; others: Jay Miller Collection)

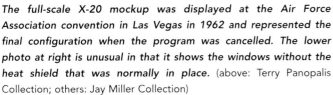

Like the X-15, the X-20 was going to use skids for its landing gear. Unlike the X-15, however, the skids on Dyna-Soar were meant to be used on concrete runways. Several later X-15 flights flew with materials proposed for Dyna-Soar to evaluate them under actual landing conditions. (NASA Dryden Flight Research Center)

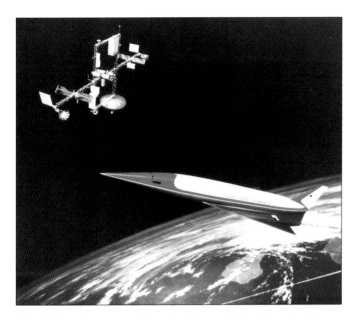

This 1987 artist concept shows the first publicly-released reference design, but is based largely on a hydrogen-fueled Boeing concept. Note the sharply-swept delta wings and single vertical stabilizer. All of the NASP concepts were deltas, but their configurations varied widely. (NASA Dryden Flight Research Center)

The program to develop what was called the National Aero-Space Plane (NASP) had its roots in a highly-classified Defense Advanced Research Projects Agency (DARPA) project called Copper Canyon that ran from 1982 to 1985. Originally conceived as a feasibility study for a single-stage-to-orbit (SSTO) vehicle that could take off and land horizontally, Copper Canyon became the starting point for what President Ronald Reagan called "... a new Orient Express that could, by the end of the next decade, take off from Dulles Airport and accelerate up to 25 times the speed of sound, attaining low earth orbit or flying to Tokyo within two hours..." It was not to be. In an ambitious program that involved every major aerospace company in the United States, DARPA proposed building a prototype NASP designated X-30. The X-30 ran into significant cost and technical difficulties and was cancelled on 27 January 1995. Although the actual funding is still classified, best guesses within the industry indicate that a little over $5.5 billion were spent on Copper Canyon and NASP-related efforts. The program estimated that an additional $17 billion would have been required before the first X-30 flight in 2001. An additional $20 billion would have been required for the first production S-30 vehicle. The Hypersonic Systems Technology Program (HySTP), initiated in late 1994, was intended to transfer the accomplishments made in hypersonic technologies by the NASP program into a technology development program. The X-43A Hyper-X is one of the results of the HySTP program.

This large model of the original X-30 reference design was later put on display in a parking lot at NASA Langley. In addition to DARPA and the contractors, the Air Force and NASA were heavily involved in the NASP program. (Tony Landis)

The X-30 model on 14 June 1990. There was a lot of debate on what fuel to use for the scramjet engines. The program initially selected liquid hydrogen, but ultimately switched to denser slush hydrogen for improved performance. (NASA Dryden Flight Research Center)

This was the reference design when the NASP program was cancelled in 1995. The 50-foot-long model was made of foam and fiberglass, weighed over 5,000 pounds, and was featured in several videos that the program released showing conceptual NASP operations. These photos were taken at NASA Langley in June 1992. (NASA Langley Research Center)

The three X-33 competitors were from Rockwell International (left), McDonnell Douglas (center), and Lockheed. The McDonnell entry was a scaled-up version of its DC-X demonstrator. The Lockheed design was the most technically challenging, and NASA would later be criticized for pushing the state-of-the-art too far. However, Lockheed was the only one of the competitors that had a follow-on commercial program defined and that was willing to contribute substantial amounts of company funds. (NASA Marshall Space Flight Center)

The Lockheed Martin X-33 was a half-scale prototype of the proposed VentureStar® reusable launch vehicle (RLV). The X-33 was designed and built as part of a "cooperative agreement" between NASA and an industry team led by Lockheed Martin that included Boeing (Rocketdyne), B. F. Goodrich (formerly Rohr Industries), Honeywell (formerly AlliedSignal), and Sverdrup. The X-33 was a suborbital demonstrator and was never intended to reach orbit. Initially the vehicle was intended to reach velocities of Mach 15, although this was later reduced to Mach 12. These speeds were chosen because they represented the worst-case aerothermal conditions expected on the way to orbit and reentry. The X-33 was designed to demonstrate unique aerospike engines, composite liquid hydrogen tanks, a metallic thermal protection system, and an austere launch site environment. The development program ran into problems almost immediately, and the failure of the composite liquid hydrogen tanks during full-scale testing led to massive cost overruns during late 2000 and early 2001. As a result, NASA declined further funding for the X-33 in March 2001 after the vehicle was about 75 percent complete. This left Lockheed, who had already invested over $200 million of company funds in the project, free to complete and fly the X-33 alone, but the company elected not to do so. The Air Force briefly expressed interest in resurrecting the program as a hypersonic demonstrator, but NASA resisted the overtures, and the uncompleted vehicle is stored at its launch site near Haystack Butte on the Edwards AFB reservation.

Reviving the same technique used for the lifting bodies, the Dryden Flight Research Center built a remote-controlled model of the X-33 and launched it using a larger remote-controlled mothership. (NASA Dryden Flight Research Center)

X-Planes Photo Scrapbook

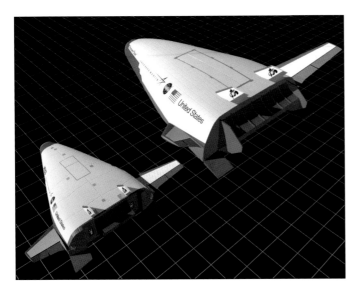

A good comparison of the X-33 (left) to the full-scale VentureStar™ that was being proposed by Lockheed. Unlike the X-33, VentureStar would be an orbital vehicle, and was envisioned being a replacement for the Space Shuttle. VentureStar would use seven large aerospike engines instead of the two J-2-based aerospikes on X-33, but was otherwise – at least at the beginning of the program – just a scaled-up version. (NASA photo by John Frassanito & Associates)

The baseline X-33 when the program began in 1996. Once wind tunnel and computer simulations provided data, the design began to change, including larger wings and vertical stabilizers. VentureStar evolved even further, losing much of the integrated wing-body shape and sprouting an external cargo pod after most internal volume was replaced by propellant tanks. (NASA photo by John Frassanito & Associates)

A 90-second test of twin linear aerospike XRS-2200 engines on 6 August 2001 at NASA Stennis. (NASA Stennis Space Center)

Test firing of a linear aerospike engine at NASA Marshall on 27 April 1997. (NASA Marshall Space Flight Center)

The flight article for the aluminum liquid oxygen tank is at left. In the middle is the structural test article for the liquid oxygen tank arriving at NASA Marshall for testing. The troublesome composite liquid hydrogen tank is at right. (Lockheed Martin)

The X-33 was being assembled in a Boeing North American facility at the southeast corner of Plant 42 in Palmdale, California, that had been used for B-1B modifications. This was done because Lockheed Skunk Works had security concerns about housing the unclassified X-33 program. (Lockheed Martin)

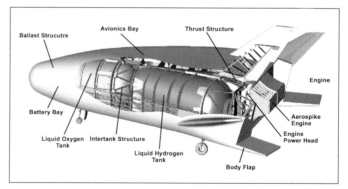

The internal arrangement of the X-33. The propellant tanks had to be oddly shaped, and initially it appeared that a composite liquid hydrogen tank structure was the most efficient method to make the desired shape. The hydrogen tank suffered from several proof-load failures and led to the program being several years behind schedule. Too late, the program decided to switch to aluminum tanks. Interestingly, NASA and Lockheed continued to refine the composite tank technology long after the X-33 had fallen by the wayside, and in mid-2004 announced they had succeeded. As many parts as possible were scrounged from other programs, such as the F-15E landing gear and the J-2S engine powerheads. (Lockheed Martin)

The structure in the foreground was the translating launch mount. The X-33 would be attached while horizontal, then rotated to the vertical launch position. (NASA Marshall Space Flight Center)

Artist concept of the X-33 launch site. One of the goals of the program was to minimize the infrastruture at the launch complex. (NASA photo by John Frassanito & Associates)

Sverdrup completed the X-33 launch site on schedule, but there was no vehicle to use it. This 1 December 1999 photo shows just how minimal the facilities were. The site is now used to store the uncompleted X-33 vehicle. (NASA Dryden photo by Carla Thomas)

The Orbital Sciences X-34 was a reusable testbed vehicle designed to demonstrate technologies that were considered essential to lowering the cost of access to space. Specific technologies to be demonstrated by the X-34 included advanced composite structures, a composite RP-1 fuel tank, an advanced thermal protection system, and autonomous flight operations. The all-composite vehicle was designed for speeds up to Mach 8 and altitudes of 250,000 feet. The first of three X-34 vehicles began captive-carry flights at Edwards AFB in June 1999 using the Lockheed L-1011 TriStar owned by Orbital Sciences. At this point the first flight was sched-uled for late 2000. The initial free flights were to be made over the White Sands Missile Range, with the full-performance flights taking place over the Atlantic Ocean off the NASA Kennedy Space Center in Florida. A special hangar was constructed at Kennedy to support the program, and was later used to house debris from the Space Shuttle Columbia accident. Although the program appeared to be progressing satisfactorily, revisions to the requirements led to significant cost growth and schedule slip. In March 2001 NASA cancelled the X-34 program before any of the aircraft had actually flown except as cargo under the L-1011.

The first X-34 was a structural test article that was not initially fitted with an engine or full-up avionics. This airframe was used for static testing, and was also carried under the L-1011 for FAA certification flights. Beginning in August 1999 it was modified at NASA Dryden to a full-up vehicle, redesignated X34A-1A, to be used for glide flights. These photos show the conversion work being performed at **NASA Dryden.** (top: NASA Dryden photo by Tom Tschida; others: NASA Dryden photos by Tony Landis)

The first airframe, X-34A-1, was used for the captive carry tests under the Lockheed L-1011. These flights began on 29 June 1999 and Orbital Sciences ultimately received a supplemental type certificate from the FAA for the mated pair. (NASA Dryden Flight Research Center)

During fit checks on the L-1011, the X-34A-1 airframe was fitted with dummy thermal protection blankets to mimic the ones that would have been used during the high-Mach flight tests. (NASA Dryden Flight Research Center)

The X-34 was not breaking any new ground performance-wise – the X-15A-2 had flown nearly as fast 30 years before – but was supposed to demonstrate technologies to make rockets cheaper and more reliable. (NASA Dryden Flight Research Center)

The X-34 takes off on its first captive carry flight on 29 June 1999 underneath the Orbital L-1011. The TriStar is used by Orbital for its commercial Pegasus missions. The X-34 is about the same size and shape as a Pegasus, so converting the L-1011 to carry the research vehicle made good sense. (NASA Dryden photo by Tom Tschida)

The X-34A-1A at the Edwards air show on 25 October 2003. Note the fictitious Air Force markings applied two days earlier. (Tony Landis)

The 60,000-lbf MC-1 Fastrac engine was being developed independently by NASA Marshall, and was the first new liquid rocket engine developed in the United States since the Space Shuttle Main Engine in the 1970s. This engine essentially duplicated the performance of the Reaction Motors XLR99 used in the X-15. (NASA Dryden photo by Tony Landis)

Left and above: *What passed for a taxi test of the X-34 was really a tow test, accomplished with the aid of a large NASA-owned truck pulling the 17,000-pound (empty) X-34 A-1. The X-34 was released at speeds up to 80 miles per hour to demonstrate the vehicle's guidance and navigation system, nose wheel steering, braking, rudder speed brake, and rudder steering.* (NASA Dryden Flight Research Center)

The second X-34 in storage at North Base on 23 January 2004. The vehicle has the flight-rated thermal protection system installed, along with the majority of the plumbing for the Fastrac engine. Note that the aerodynamic control surfaces are missing. The wingtip of the first vehicle is barely visible at right. Most spare parts for the program are in boxes nearby. (Tony Landis)

When the program ended, the first X-34 was placed into temporary storage at NASA Dryden. The second aircraft had never been at Dryden. Both aircraft are now in storage in an Air Force building on North Base at Edwards (see above). Note the two cranked-wing F-16XLs in the background. (NASA Dryden photo by Tony Landis)

X-Planes Photo Scrapbook

Artist concept of the X-37 in the Space Shuttle Orbiter payload bay. The X-37 would be deployed from the payload bay, spend several days in orbit, then autonomously reenter the atmosphere and land at *Edwards*. (Boeing)

The X-37 Approach and Landing Test Vehicle under construction. The vehicle was relatively small, being only 27.5 feet long and spanning 15 feet. These dimensions (particularly the wing span) were dictated by the size of the shuttle payload bay. (Boeing photos by Rod Davis)

The X-37, formerly known as the Future-X Pathfinder, was intended to make a series of atmospheric and orbital test flights to evaluate airframe, propulsion, and operations technologies designed to lower the cost of access to space. These included a highly durable, high-temperature thermal protection system. The X-37 was to be launched aboard the Space Shuttle as a secondary payload – once on-orbit the Space Shuttle will deploy the X-37 from the payload bay. The vehicle is designed to be capable of at least 20 flights and landings. The X-37 shape was identical to the X-40A developed for the Air Force, and the two programs were merged with the lone X-40A serving as a prototype for the X-37. The Approach and Landing Test Vehicle successfully completed structural testing in Huntington Beach, California, in mid-2004. Initially the plan included orbital flights by 2002, but as of mid-2004 the schedule called for atmospheric flight tests of the Approach and Landing Test Vehicle in late 2004 and orbital tests in 2006.

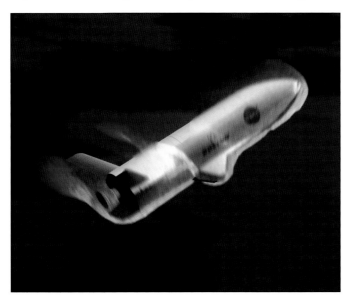

One of the items the X-37 is supposed to demonstrate is an advanced thermal protection system that does not rely on the fragile ceramic tiles used by the Space Shuttle Orbiter. (Boeing)

Artist rendering of the X-37 being released from the Space Shuttle on-orbit. This was considered a low-risk procedure since the shuttle has launched dozens of satellites and other free-flyers. (Boeing)

Fictitious Air Force markings on the X-37 mockup at NASA Dryden on 28 April 2003. (NASA Dryden Flight Research Center)

The X-37 mockup next to the X-40A on 22 June 2000, illustrating their size difference. (NASA Dryden Flight Research Center)

The SV-5J (X-24A) that had been on display at the Air Force Academy in Colorado was loaned to Scaled Composites to make a mold for the X-38. The mold was modified into the actual shape of the X-38 and the composite shell was made from it. This is the mold on 11 August 1995. (NASA Dryden photo by Carla Thomas)

As part of the U.S. portion of the International Space Station, NASA agreed to supply a vehicle capable of bringing home four astronauts in the event of an emergency on the ISS (the other three astronauts of a seven-man crew would be brought home by a Russian Soyuz). NASA originally called the crew rescue vehicle the X-35 – the first X-designation actually assigned by the space agency – not realizing that the Air Force had already assigned that number. The X-38 was a concept demonstrator of a crew rescue vehicle (previously called an assured crew return vehicle – ACRV) for the International Space Station. The vehicles were designed in-house by the NASA Johnson Space Center with assistance from the Dryden Flight Research Center, and were manufactured by Scaled Composites. The X-38 design used the SV-5 lifting body shape originally developed by Martin Marietta for the X-24A in the mid-1960s. Following the jettison of a deorbit engine module, the X-38 would glide from orbit unpowered like the Space Shuttle and then use a steerable parafoil parachute, a technology developed by the Army, for its final descent to landing. The first X-38, known as Vehicle 131, arrived at Dryden on 4 June 1997 and made its maiden flight in March 1998. The second vehicle, V132, was delivered to Dryden in September 1998 and made four unpowered drop tests. Unfortunately, the X-38 program was cancelled in late 2002 before a space-rated vehicle had been assembled. Both completed airframes are in storage at the NASA Johnson Space Center in Houston.

The first X-38 (V-131) under assembly at Scaled Composites on 6 August 1996. The X-24A influence is clearly seen in the shape of the canopy. (NASA Dryden Flight Research Center)

The people at NASA Dryden posed the newest lifting body with the oldest. Here is the first X-38 and the M2-F1 together on 27 August 1997. (NASA Dryden Flight Research Center)

X-Planes Photo Scrapbook

V-131R drops away from NB-52B on its third and final flight on 13 December 2001. Note the simple pylon under the NB-52 wing compared to the large structures used by the X-15 and lifting bodies. (NASA Dryden photo by Carla Thomas)

X-38 V-132 in the Space Shuttle hangar at NASA Dryden on 18 April 1999. Note the X-34 A-1 in the background. The object just behind the X-38 is a disassembled tailcone fairing for the Space Shuttle Orbiter. (NASA Dryden Flight Research Center)

V-132 at NASA Dryden in 1998. Note the unusual NASA insignia on the nose and tail used by NASA Johnson on some aircraft. The vehicle is being lifted off the white blocks at the left (see photo to the right for example). (NASA Dryden Flight Research Center)

Both X-38s together at NASA Dryden on the day that V-132 was delivered (10 September 1998). At this point the shape of both vehicles was fairly true to the SV-5/X-24A. Note the body flap on V-131 in the background. (NASA Dryden Flight Research Center)

The initial X-38 scale model was tested during August 1995 at California City airport, very near the Scaled Composite facility in *Mojave.* (NASA Dryden photo by Jim Ross)

First flight of X-38 V-131 on 12 March 1998. The parasail was housed in a compartment on the aft deck of the vehicle. Note that *one cell of the parasail is torn.* (NASA Dryden photo by Carla Thomas)

X-38 V-132 glides during its second free flight on 9 July 1999. Note the deflected body flap. (NASA Dryden Flight Research Center)

X-38 V-131R on the lakebed after its third and final flight on 13 December 2001. (NASA Dryden Flight Research Center)

V-131 on 16 March 1998. Note the blunt trailing edge on the fin tips and the empty location that would hold a de-orbit engine on the actual spacecraft. (NASA Dryden Flight Research Center)

V-131 under the wing of the NB-52B on 6 July 1997. The X-38 did not have any propulsion or pressurization systems that required connecting to the B-52. (NASA Dryden photo by Tony Landis)

V-131R parked in front of the mate/demate device at NASA Dryden with the Space Shuttle Orbiter Discovery (OV-103) being readied for a ferry flight after STS-92. The photo was taken on 30 October 2000. (NASA Dryden photo by Tony Landis)

Great view of V-131 under the wing of the NB-52B on 19 November 1997. Note the wing flex on the Boeing bomber, a very natural occurrence. The sway braces between the pylon and X-38 were large structures. (NASA Dryden Flight Research Center)

The X-40A undergoing maintenance at NASA Dryden on 27 June 2000. Panels along the top of the fuselage allowed easy access to most systems in the vehicle. (NASA Dryden Flight Research Center)

The Boeing X-40A was an 80-percent-scale version of the proposed Space Maneuver Vehicle (SMV) that became the X-37. The SMV was designed to deliver small satellites, perform on-orbit reconnaissance, and other duties. The X-40A completed a successful autonomous approach and landing on its first flight test on 11 August 1998 after being dropped from an Army UH-60 Black Hawk helicopter at an altitude of 9,000 feet over the White Sands Missile Range. The vehicle used an integrated INS/GPS to touch down on a hard surface runway. After its single test flight, the Air Force gave the X-40A to NASA for use as a prototype of the X-37 vehicle, and the X-40A arrived at the NASA Dryden Flight Research Center on 26 May 2000. In a concurrent test program to support the low-speed atmospheric flight dynamics of the X-37 design, the X-40A successfully completed its test program with seven successful flights at Edwards. During the series of flights, the unmanned X-40A was released from a CH-47 Chinook helicopter at 15,000 feet, and it autonomously acquired the runway and landed in a mode similar to a conventional aircraft. The X-40A demonstrated the guidance, navigation & control algorithms, software, calculated air data system, integrated GPS/INS, and aerodynamic performance of the basic X-37, and also used its mobile flight operations control center. The X-40A is currently in storage at the Boeing facility in Seal Beach, California.

The X-40A made seven successful flights at Edwards, including Free Flight 4A on 5 May 2001. Interestingly, NASA markings did not appear on the X-40A, even after the space agency took over the program from the Air Force. (NASA Dryden photo by Tom Tschida)

X-40A poses with Space Shuttle Orbiter Endeavour on 1 May 2001. The basic X-40 shape was very similar to several that were investigated and rejected during the development of Space Shuttle. (NASA Dryden photo by Tony Landis)

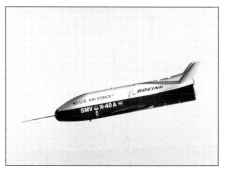

X-40A being carried by the CH-47D during Free Flight 3 on 26 April 2001. (NASA Dryden photos by Jim Ross)

X-40 Free Flight 5 on 8 May 2001. (NASA Dryden photos by Jim Ross)

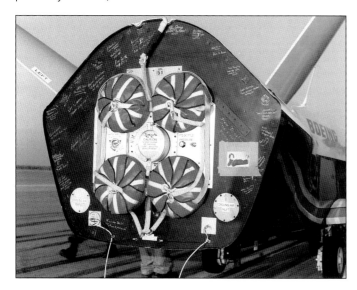

The four parachute packs on the back of the X-40A. Note that each member of the test team signed the back of the vehicle prior to its last flight on 19 May 2001. (NASA Dryden Flight Research Center)

The X-40 test team poses in front of the CH-47D carrier helicopter, T-34C chase plane, and X-40A used during the program at NASA Dryden. (NASA Dryden Flight Research Center)

REALLY WEIRD

Artist concept of the LLRV from September 1963. (NASA Dryden Flight Research Center)

Above and right: *An LLRV on the lakebed on 20 August 1960. The LLRV had a tubular metal framework with sheet-metal truss construction surrounding a 4,200-lbf General Electric CF700-2V turbojet engine. The jet was attached to a large movable gimbal that permitted the engine and the framework to move independently. Flight control was accomplished using a combination of the jet engine and hydrogen-peroxide thrusters.* (NASA Dryden Flight Research Center)

All of the time and expense lavished upon the Apollo lunar missions ultimately hinged upon the last few minutes before the Lunar Module landed on the Moon. The first landing would be an entirely new experience for any astronaut, and it had to be perfect, so a lot of training was in order. The Lunar Module was designed for vertical landing and takeoff, and was able to briefly hover and fly horizontally before landing. At first glance it seemed that a helicopter could be used to simulate flying the LM, but early test flights proved that it was not even close. Helicopters, or any aircraft, were subject to the influences of winds, air temperature, and the Earth's gravity. In order to simulate flying near the Moon, the flight vehicle had to automatically nullify the effects of nature so it would behave as if it were operating in a vacuum, and it had to respond as if it were subject to the much lighter lunar gravity. Ideas for this unique type of flying machine began circulating at the NASA Flight Research Center in early 1961. By the end of the year, it awarded a study contract to Bell Aerosystems based on that company's history of vertical takeoff research airplanes. On 1 February 1963 Bell received a contract to design and fabricate two Lunar Lander Research Vehicles (LLRV) that were ultimately delivered during April 1964. By mid-1966, NASA had accumulated enough data from the LLRV flight program to order three Lunar Landing Training Vehicles for the NASA Manned Spacecraft Center (now the Johnson Space Center) to train the Apollo astronauts. The original LLRVs were subsequently modified to the LLTV configuration and used in Houston as well.

The jet engine was controlled automatically to simulate flight within the lunar environment. Aerodynamic drag forces were opposed with vectored thrust so the vehicle would respond as though in a vacuum, and the jet supported five-sixths of the vehicle's weight to simulate lunar gravity. After the jet engine had throttled-up enough to simulate lunar gravity, the LLRV's vertical movements were controlled by two rockets mounted in the center, next to the jet. There were also six emergency lift rockets that could also be used in the event of a jet engine failure. (NASA Dryden Flight Research Center)

The pilot sat on a Weber ejection seat. The LLRV was initially flown using a conventional stick-and-rudder-pedal system but later changed to a collective and side stick controller as shown in the photo at right. (NASA Dryden Flight Research Center)

The rudimentary cockpit originally installed on the LLRVs was eventually replaced by something that more closely resembled an LM. The pilot, however, remained seated, although the LM was flown standing up. (NASA Dryden Flight Research Center)

Fuel constraints limited most flights to about 10 minutes, but a lunar-landing-simulation maneuver could be done in just two minutes. Pilots described the feeling of flying in the lunar mode as one of "slow motion" compared to earth mode VTOL operation. Large attitude angles were required to start or stop horizontal flight, while a lot of lead-time was needed to slow the vehicle over a specific spot. The pilots were forced to operate at much steeper attitudes, and for longer duration, than required for conventional VTOL operation. Note the angle of the jet engine as the LLRV maneuvers. (NASA Dryden Flight Research Center)

The Paresev (Paraglider Research Vehicle) was an indirect outgrowth of kite-parachute studies by NACA Langley engineer Francis M. Rogallo. In the early 1960s, the "Rogallo wing" seemed an excellent means of returning a spacecraft to Earth, and in May 1961, the NASA Space Task Group contracted with North American to study an inflatable Rogallo-type "Parawing" for spacecraft. The Paresev was used to gain in-flight experience with four different membranes (wings), and was not used to develop the more complicated inflatable deployment system. The Paresev completed nearly 350 flights during a research program from 1962 until 1964. (NASA Dryden Flight Research Center)

The oblique wing was thought to offer the supersonic transport twice the fuel economy of an aircraft with more conventional wings. Also called a "scissors" wing, it was an offshoot of the variable-sweep-wing concept, which was first investigated with the X-5. The oblique wing on the AD-1 pivoted about the fuselage, remaining perpendicular to it during slow flight and swinging to angles of up to 60 degrees as aircraft speed increased. The twin turbojet, piloted AD-1 (left) was flown 79 times between 1979 and 1982. Although the oblique wing is still considered a viable concept for large transports, the unpleasant flying characteristics of the AD-1 at extreme wing-sweep angles may have discouraged aircraft designers from adopting this configuration. (NASA Dryden Flight Research Center)

PROTOTYPES

A model of the proposed X-6 showing the P-1 atomic powerplant's four X40 engines under the mid-fuselage. The atomic reactor would have been located in bomb bay No. 4 immediately above them. (Lockheed Martin via the Jay Miller Collection)

Two Convair X-6s were ordered to evaluate the operational practicality of airborne nuclear propulsion systems prior to committing to building a prototype of a dedicated military design such as WS-125A. The specific areas to be tested included crew shielding, propulsion, radiobiology, and the effects of radiation on various aircraft systems. In addition to the X-6s, a single NB-36H was ordered to serve as an early flyable testbed. In the NB-36H, the nuclear reactor was functioning but provided no power to the aircraft itself. The X-6s would have been powered by a prototype airborne nuclear propulsion system installed in the aft bomb bay. The United States invested over $1 billion during the 1950s and 1960s toward developing atomic-powered aircraft. A dedicated test facility was constructed in Connecticut, and an operating powerplant was built in the deserts of Idaho. The Strategic Air Command even issued a requirement for an atomic-powered supersonic bomber called WS-125A. But it was all for naught. In the end, the X-6 program was cancelled before either of the two aircraft were built. The NB-36H was completed, however, making its first flight in September 1955. After conducting tests for approximately two years, the nuclear reactor was removed and the NB-36H was scrapped at Carswell AFB, Texas.

The NB-36H was a modified B-36 that carried an operating nuclear reactor to evaluate the radiation shielding requirements of an atomic-powered airplane under real-world conditions. The reactor provided no power to the aircraft. (Lockheed Martin)

The X-9 Shrike (also designated the RTV-A-4) will remain perhaps the least heralded of all the early X-vehicles. Designed to serve as a test-bed for the ill-fated GAM-63 RASCAL air-to-surface missile, the X-9 was doomed to an unspectacular, but nevertheless productive, flight test career. The intent was to obtain aerodynamic, stability, guidance system, and propulsion data prior to proceeding into full-scale development of the RASCAL. Although 93 X-9s were initially ordered, only 31 were actually delivered. None survived, and the only remaining identifiable piece is a large part of a vertical stabilizer in the Larry Bell Museum in Mentone, Indiana.

An X-9 is launched from an EB-50D on 16 December 1952 over the White Sands Missile Range. Note that the trapeze in the bomb bay has not retracted yet. (Bell Aerospace via the Jay Miller Collection)

Three photos of X-9 Shrike missiles. The one in the center is being loaded into an EB-50D carrier aircraft. The missile was 22.75 feet long, 22 inches in diameter, and weighed 3,495 pounds fully loaded. (Bell Aerospace via the Jay Miller Collection)

The X-9 led to the GAM-63 RASCAL. Here is one of the YDB-47Bs (51-2186) from the 447th Bomb Squadron at Pinecastle AFB, Florida, with a GAM-63 RASCAL missile. The first launch of a guided RASCAL took place in October 1953 from a DB-47 director aircraft. The GAM-63 program was terminated in late 1958, shortly before the first RASCAL-equipped SAC unit was to become operational, in favor of the more promising and longer-range (but slower) Hound Dog missile carried by the B-52. (Terry Panopalis Collection)

The North American Aviation X-10 was an aerodynamic and systems testbed for the cruise component of the SM-64 (B-64) Navaho missile. The X-10 was powered by a pair of Westinghouse J40 turbojet engines that could push the 42,000-pound missile to over Mach 2. At a later date, the X-10 itself was considered a cruise missile candidate, armed with a nuclear warhead and capable of taking off and flying to its target under its own power – but the successful development of the Atlas and Titan intercontinental ballistic missiles (ICBM) eliminated the need for such a weapon. The X-10 successfully contributed to the development of the much larger Navaho missile, although that program would subsequently be cancelled in favor of the rocket-powered ICBMs. The X-10 verified the aerodynamics of the cruise component of the Navaho, as well as its complex navigation system. Thirteen X-10s were manufactured, but only ten were flown. The missiles had retractable tricycle landing gear and were recoverable. Flight testing took place at Edwards AFB and Cape Canaveral. A single X-10 survived and is now displayed at the Air Force Museum. An SM-65 Navaho missile is on display outside the gate at the Cape Canaveral AFS, Florida.

The first X-10 with the rear fuselage panels removed showing the two Westinghouse J40-WE-1 turbojets. The "19307" appears to be a "guided missile" number (GM-19307) and not an official serial number. (Boeing Historical Archives)

A great view of the first X-10 showing the shape of the canards. (Boeing Historical Archives)

Many of the X-10s were used more than once and this one, at least, had mission marks painted on it. (Boeing Historical Archives)

X-Planes Photo Scrapbook

The first – and last – flight of the third X-10. The vehicle was destroyed because the self-destruct package had been inadvertently wired to the landing gear retract switch. (Boeing Historical Archives)

The hangar at Edwards showing three X-10s undergoing maintenance. Note the empty engine bays on the two facing away from the photographer and the early electronic test equipment at the lower left. (Boeing Historical Archives)

The first X-10 received a red photo tracking stripe down the entire length of its fuselage while at Edwards. The landing gear was fragile and brake failures were fairly common, although the drag chute helped matters somewhat. (Boeing Historical Archives)

The second X-10 in flight showing the clipped-tip delta wing and outward canting vertical stabilizers. The X-10 was a faithful subscale reproduction of the ramjet-powered SM-64 Navaho cruise missile. (Boeing Historical Archives)

The color has shifted somewhat over the years, but this is how the first X-10 looked when it arrived at Edwards in mid-1953. This aircraft managed to survive the test program and is currently on display at the Air Force Museum. (Boeing Historical Archives)

When the Atlas ICBM was being developed, Convair proposed constructing two incremental test vehicles to assist in verifying the enormous technological developments necessary to complete the program. At this point Atlas was envisioned as an enormous 160-foot high, 12-foot diameter missile weighing 440,000 pounds and powered by four booster engines and a single sustainer engine. The first of these test vehicles was the X-11. Using an incremental flight test program, the X-11 would test the overall airframe using only the single sustainer engine while the subsequent X-12 would integrate more components including the four booster engines. In the meantime, the National Laboratories made breakthrough discoveries that allowed the nuclear payload for the Atlas to be drastically reduced in size. Based on the new estimates, Convair significantly reduced the size and weight of the Atlas ICBM, allowing the use of only three engines (two boosters and one sustainer) instead of the original five. The X-11 fell by the wayside. Still, Convair wanted to proceed with an incremental test program, but this time the resultant vehicle was called the Atlas Series A (later shortened to simply Atlas A) instead of X-11. The test missile would be powered by the two booster engines; the sustainer would be added on the later Atlas B (which took the place of the X-12). In the end, 16 Atlas As were built and 8 were launched from Cape Canaveral (left). The Atlas B was generally similar to the earlier Atlas A but incorporated the planned sustainer engine to prove the stage-and-a-half concept. A total of 13 Atlas Bs were manufactured for flight and ground tests (right). All of the basic subsystems were tested in this series, including the MA-1 propulsion system, the Mod 1 radio guidance system, and the Mark 2 heat-sink reentry vehicle. The Atlas B series demonstrated booster staging and reentry vehicle separation, and attained a range of 6,500 miles with vehicle 12B. They successfully demonstrated the pressure-stabilized propellant tanks and propulsion system components destined to equip the Atlas ICBM – which later became one of the premier space launch vehicles. (45th Space Wing History Office Collection)

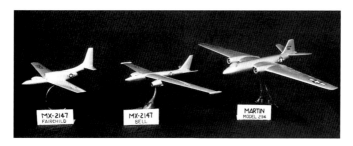

The three contenders for MX-2147 were the Fairchild M-195 (left), Bell Model 67 (center), and the Martin Model 294. These models are not to scale, as the Bell aircraft had a wingspan considerably longer than the Martin entry. The Model 294 would go on to become the RB-57D. All of these designs would be eclipsed by the success of the Lockheed U-2, which has been in operational service (in various models) for 50 years. (Bell Aerospace via the Jay Miller Collection)

The Bell X-16 was not so much a prototype as it was supposed to be an operational high-altitude long-range reconnaissance aircraft. A total of 28 aircraft were ordered, but none would be completed before the Lockheed U-2 successfully demonstrated its ability to perform the spy mission. The first X-16 was reportedly over 80 percent complete when it was cancelled. The X-16 was a designer's nightmare – the wing was an extremely long-span high-aspect ratio unit that was significantly lighter and more flexible than any in existence at the time. In fact, the entire airframe was extremely flexible, the result of the need to make the aircraft as light as possible to allow it to achieve its 70,000-foot mission altitude. A 3,000-mile unrefueled range was predicted for the production aircraft. Although never built, the X-16 pioneered several notable advances in lightweight structure design, and was also the driving force behind the development of high-altitude versions of the J57 jet engine that would go on to power the U-2 and other aircraft.

An early model of the X-16 showing wingtip-mounted outrigger landing gear and preliminary engine nacelles. The landing gear would be moved to a mid-span location so that the aircraft could use available runways. (Bell Aerospace via the Jay Miller Collection)

The X-16 mockup under construction in temporary structure at Bell's Wheatfield, New York, plant. The relative size of the aircraft can be determined by comparing it with the men in the background. (Bell Aerospace via the Jay Miller Collection)

The Lockheed X-27 Lancer program can trace its roots to a Lockheed desire to develop a replacement for the F-104 Starfighter that was in wide service around the world. Lockheed's goal was to create a new aircraft with considerably improved performance while maintaining significant commonality with the F-104 to ease maintenance and training concerns. The X-27 was conceived as the prototype of the desired advanced lightweight fighter and was based on the CL-1200 Lancer design developed by the Lockheed Skunk Works. The program, however, failed to obtain any significant congressional or DoD support, and no actual aircraft were built. Nevertheless, a full-scale mockup was completed. In the end, the X-27 program was a lesson in political maneuvering as much as technological advances. Lockheed's Kelly Johnson almost managed to get official backing of a commercial program, but was ultimately defeated by military services that did not want to see competition for the funding necessary to complete the F-14 and F-15 programs. Eventually the Air Force and Navy would embrace the lightweight fighter concept with the F-16 and (sort of) F/A-18, but Lockheed would not be a participant.

A later version of the X-27 mockup showing the revised inlets for the TF30 turbofan. The CL-1200 was considerably longer than an F-104 to house additional fuel. Note the Lancer logo and the small Skunk Works emblem on the aft fuselage. (Lockheed Martin)

The original CL-1200 mockup used the forward fuselage from the F-104G mockup, and looked much like the improved Starfighter that it was. Note that the horizontal stabilizer has been moved from on top of the vertical to the bottom of the fuselage. The CL-1200 increased internal fuel by over 50 percent. In this configuration the mockup used the same half-cone inlets the F-104 had used for its General Electric J79 turbojet. When the decision was made to switch to the Pratt & Whitney TF30, the inlets changed considerably. (Lockheed Martin)

The X-32A in final assembly at the Boeing facility in Palmdale, California. Almost all of the skin was composite material. (Boeing)

The X-32A showing the open weapons bay door with a clipped-wing AIM-120C air-to-air missile inside. (Boeing)

The Pratt & Whitney JSF119-614 propulsion system for the STOVL X-32B on a test stand in Palm Beach, Florida. Note the rotating nozzles in the center of the engine. The main exhaust was equipped with a two-dimensional thrust-vectoring nozzle. (Pratt & Whitney)

The X-32B cockpit on 26 April 2001. The cockpit used components from a variety of aircraft, notably the F/A-18, to minimize costs during the demonstration program. A conventional center stick was retained instead of a side-stick controller. (Tony Landis)

The X-32B performs a vertical landing at NAS Patuxent River, Maryland. The rotating nozzles for vertical lift are inside the fuselage compartment with the open doors just forward of the main landing gear. Small nozzles at each wingtip provide roll control. A great deal of equipment – gear actuators, inlet cowl, refueling probe, and more – had to be removed from the X-32 to bring its weight down enough to perform vertical operations. (Boeing)

X-Planes Photo Scrapbook

The Joint Strike Fighter (JSF) has been described as the largest single defense program in history, with a potential market for 5,000-8,000 aircraft worth over $200 billion when all potential export orders are included. In November 1996, Boeing and Lockheed Martin were awarded contracts to build two Concept Demonstrator Aircraft (CDA) – one CTOL (conventional takeoff and landing) version and one STOVL (short takeoff and vertical landing) version – each. The aircraft were not intended to be fighter prototypes, but rather to prove that the selected design concepts would work, hence the use of X designations. Boeing was assigned X-32 (a number reserved for the earlier JAST program) while Lockheed Martin received the designation X-35. The Boeing X-32 used a novel airframe shape combined with a direct-lift STOVL configuration. The Harrier-style direct lift concept required the lift nozzles to be on the center of gravity of the aircraft. To achieve this, the engine was located in the front portion of the fuselage, with the vectoring nozzles immediately behind it, and then a long exhaust duct led back to the afterburner and pitch-axis thrust vectoring nozzle at the rear. The engine position and overall dimension limitations dictated a very short nose. For the two CDA aircraft, the designation X-32A was allocated to the CTOL version and X-32B to the STOVL version. Unlike the Lockheed Martin X-35, there were no airframe changes required to demonstrate U.S. Navy aircraft carrier (CV) approach capabilities – the X-32A performed both roles. The X-32A featured a non-moving intake and wide span wings with accentuated tip extensions. The X-32B featured a moving intake cowl that translat-

ed forward during hover to allow more air into the engine. The fuselage was slightly shorter, and the wing span was narrower to reduced weight. After the X-32 design was frozen, the planned Model 375 production version continued to evolve, gaining a conventional horizontal stabilizer and a stubby swept wing rather than the original delta wing. The engine intake cowl was also raked backward rather than forward. The Lockheed Martin X-35 was selected as the winning JSF design on 26 October 2001. Some F-35 work may be awarded to Boeing as a consolation. The X-32s will eventually be donated to museums.

The 737-200 Avionics Flying Laboratory fitted with a 48-inch nose and radome assembly to the forward pressure bulkhead of the aircraft was used to integrate and test the advanced avionics for the Boeing Joint Strike Fighter (JSF) demonstrators. (Boeing)

The X-32A over Edwards during its 17th test flight with its in-flight refueling probe extended. To underscore the commonality of its design, Boeing used the X-32A to demonstrate both the CTOL and CV handling qualities. (U.S. Air Force photo by Steve Zapka)

The X-32B STOVL demonstrator in flight giving a good view of the two-dimensional main exhaust nozzle. The rotating forward exhaust nozzles are behind the dark doors in the middle of the fuselage. (U.S. Air Force photo by Steve Zapka)

A model of the Engineering and Manufacturing Development (EMD) airplane shows that it was considerably different from the demonstrators. Note the horizontal stabilizers and revised wing shape. The inlet was also significantly different. (Boeing)

Compare the wing shape of the X-32A with the EMD model at left. Also note that there are no horizontal stabilizers on the demonstrator aircraft. These significant changes largely invalidated the intent of the demonstration program. (U.S. Air Force photo by Steve Zapka)

An almost unanimous opinion among aviation enthusiasts is that the X-32 is the single ugliest aircraft to be built by an American manufacturer in recent memory. As it turned out, production aircraft would have born little resemblance to the two demonstrators. (U.S. Air Force photo by Steve Zapka)

Although the two aircraft have very little in common, the X-35 and F-22 share a family resemblance of sorts. Note the faceted air intake to minimize the radar cross-section, although the canopy installation is relatively conventional, unlike the F-117. (Lockheed Martin)

Before being painted, the X-35 was a patchwork quilt of different metals and composites. Note the large black covers on top of the fuselage where the lift fan and air intakes go for the STOVL version. (Lockheed Martin)

The first X-35 (301) during an engine test in Palmdale on 17 August 2000. The X-35 uses a convergent-divergent main exhaust nozzle instead of the two-dimensional nozzle used by the X-32. (Lockheed Martin photo by Marty Wolin)

The X-35B (also aircraft 301) STOVL demonstrator with the lift fan doors and auxiliary intakes open during Flight 42 on 11 July 2001. (Lockheed Martin photo by Tom Reynolds)

The X-35B flies formation with the only operational vertical takeoff aircraft, the Harrier. This provides a good size comparison between the two aircraft. (Lockheed Martin photo by Tom Reynolds)

The X-35B in full vertical mode during Flight 48 on 16 July 2001, performing the first vertical landing of the program. The pilot was Simon Hargreaves from BAe, somebody well experienced in landing the Harrier. (Lockheed Martin photo by Denny Lombard)

The X-35 was the Lockheed Martin Joint Strike Fighter (JSF) demonstrator, competing with the Boeing X-32. Lockheed constructed two prototypes for the evaluation. The initial X-35A reflected the basic Air Force CTOL design, and was used for early flights before being modified into the STOVL version, designated X-35B. While Boeing proposed a direct lift STOVL design based on that used in the Harrier, Lockheed opted for a different approach in meeting the vertical flight requirements. Inspired by the Russian Yak-141, the X-35B incorporated a separate lift-fan that was shaft-driven by the F119 engine, allowing cooler exhaust temperatures during hover. While the Boeing design was more conventional, Lockheed argued that its strategy was better in the long term since it offered more room for growth as the aircraft evolves. The second airframe was the X-35C STOVL demonstrator for the Navy. This model featured an enlarged wing of greater span and area for larger fuel capacity as well as enlarged horizontal tails and flaperons for greater control effectiveness during low-speed carrier approaches. The X-35 was selected as the winner of the JSF competition on 26 October 2001. The production aircraft, unexplainably, will be designated F-35. The System Development and Demonstration (SDD) phase of the F-35 JSF program started with the signing of the SDD contract in October 2001, with the delivery of test aircraft scheduled to begin in 2008. During the SDD phase, 22 aircraft (14 flying test aircraft and 8 ground-test aircraft) will be produced and tested. The JSF program is slated to produce a total of 3,002 aircraft for the United States' and United Kingdom's armed forces, and possibly additional aircraft for new members Italy, Turkey, Canada, Denmark, Norway, and the Netherlands. Other countries have expressed an interest in joining the program and are expected to do so in the coming years. The program is potentially worth $200 billion after all the export orders are considered.

The X-32 (left) and X-35 pose together at Edwards. (Lockheed Martin)

The X-35C (300) used larger wing and tail surfaces, and was the air-craft carrier compatibility demonstrator. The basic wing carry-through structure was common between all variants. (Lockheed Martin photo by Tom Reynolds)

Unlike the Harrier and X-32, Lockheed decided use a shaft-driven Rolls-Royce lift fan in the STOVL version. The exhaust from this fan is significantly cooler than the exhaust from the nozzles on the Harrier and X-32. (Lockheed Martin)

The larger wing of the X-35C provides more lift for carrier opera-tions. All versions of the X-35 use flaperons, but only the X-35C was equipped with ailerons. The other wingtips fold upward for carrier storage. (Lockheed Martin photo by David Drais)

The large exhaust nozzle dominates the rear view of the aircraft and seemingly will make an excellent target for infrared-guided surface-to-air missiles. Otherwise the aircraft is well equipped with stealth design concepts. (Boeing via the Gerald H. Balzer Collection)

WITHOUT PILOTS

The first X-36 during Flight 25. Somewhere around Flight 21, additional markings were added to the aircraft. Small markings near the exhaust and both gear doors had "X-36-1," and mission markings were put on the lower left side of the front fuselage. Just prior to Flight 25 the names of two 'pilots' were added – "Stick" and "Rudder." Also a red arrow was added on the upper fuselage with the warning "Rocket Installed." (NASA Dryden photo by Carla Thomas)

The 28-percent-scale, remotely piloted Boeing X-36 had no vertical or horizontal tails, reducing the weight, drag, and radar cross section typically associated with traditional fighter aircraft. The X-36 also explored advanced flight control technologies, such as split ailerons and thrust vectoring. Boeing (formerly McDonnell Douglas) manufactured two X-36 vehicles, and the aircraft successfully completed all of its planned low- and high-g agility maneuvers, which demonstrated the aircraft's ability to quickly perform under a wide range of aerodynamic loads, and included 360-degree rolls at angles of attack (AoA) up to 15 degrees and rapid turning-rolling maneuvers at up to 35 degrees AoA. Including the design and production of the two aircraft and flight testing, the total budget for the X-36 program was only $17 million. The unmanned aircraft completed 33 flights between May 1997 and December 1998. The X-36 hardware and software, avionics, flight controls and Williams International F112 engine have been reused for Boeing's X-50 canard rotor/wing demonstrator.

Both X-36s pose together at NASA Dryden on 10 December 1997. The second vehicle never flew and was only taxied once.. Ship two was never flown and only taxied once. Note the mission marks on the first aircraft (right). (NASA Dryden photo by Tony Landis)

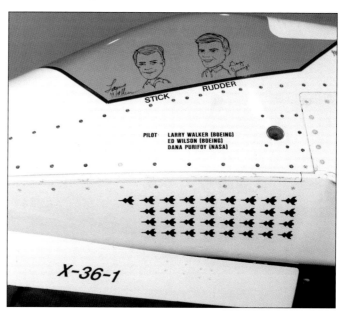

Mission markings on the first X-36. Note the "stick" and "rudder" pilots. (NASA Dryden Flight Research Center)

The X-45 was developed by the Boeing (former McDonnell Douglas) Phantom Works in St. Louis, Missouri. The X-45 unmanned combat air vehicle (UCAV) is a tailless, 27-foot-long, jet-powered aircraft with a 34-foot wingspan. The vehicle incorporates a thrust vectoring system for yaw control, thus eliminating the need for vertical stabilizers, reducing the drag and radar cross-section. The UCAV System Demonstration Program is a joint DARPA/USAF/Boeing effort to demonstrate the technical feasibility for a UCAV system to conduct various strike missions within the emerging global command and control architecture. The demonstrations will provide the information necessary to enable decision-makers to determine whether it is technically and fiscally prudent to continue development of a production UCAV. Two X-45A aircraft completed 16 flights during Phase I testing, which ended in February 2003. Initial plans for an X-45B version were apparently cancelled in mid-2003, with the program moving directly to a more capable X-45C due to a change in mission requirements.

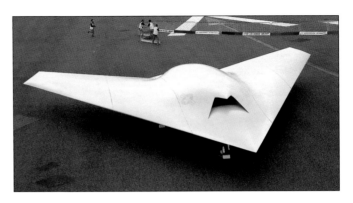

A full-scale model of the X-45C was unveiled at the Farnborough International Air Show in July 2004. Newly renamed the Joint Unmanned Combat Air Systems (J-UCAS), the X-45C is scheduled to be completed in 2006 with a first flight in 2007. (DARPA)

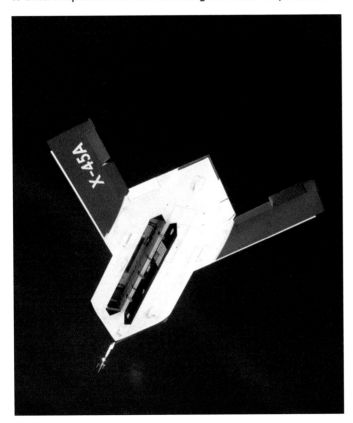

Boeing operated a very sharp-looking T-33 in support of the X-45 program. Here it is with the first X-45 on 11 July 2002. (NASA Dryden Flight Research Center)

The first X-45 during Flight 13 on 21 February 2001. Note the open weapons bay and the large American flag inside. (NASA Dryden photo by Lori Losey)

Both X-45s on display during UCAV media day at NASA Dryden on 11 July 2002. Note that the first vehicle had blue trim while the second was finished in red. (NASA Dryden Flight Research Center)

The Northrop Grumman X-47A Pegasus is another potential UCAV, this time for the U.S. Navy. Designed with stealth features and shaped like a kite, Pegasus is constructed largely with composite materials. One of the first tasks of the Pegasus flight program will be to demonstrate acceptable aerodynamic flying qualities suitable for operations from an aircraft carrier. Northrop Grumman is performing trade studies, analysis and preliminary design for a UCAV-N under a $2 million contract with DARPA and the U.S. Navy. The goal of the joint DARPA/Navy project is to demonstrate the technical feasibility for a UCAV system to effectively and affordably conduct sea-based surveillance, suppression of enemy air defenses, and strike missions within the emerging global command and control architecture.

The first flight of the X-47A at NWC China Lake on 23 February 2003. (Northrop Grumman photos by Bruce Wartlieb)

The first engine run on the X-47A was conducted in the parking lot of the Northrop Grumman facility on 8 December 2001. (Northrop Grumman photo by Tony Chong)

In June 1998 a $24 million agreement between DARPA and The Boeing Company funded a 37-month effort by the Boeing Phantom Works to design, build, and fly two technology demonstrators to assess and validate the X-50 Dragonfly Canard Rotor/Wing (CRW) advanced rotorcraft. The unmanned X-50A CRW is 17.7 feet long, 6.5 feet high, and the rotor blades have a diameter of 12 feet. Powered by a conventional turbofan engine, the X-50A used diverter valves to direct thrust to the rotor blade tips (for helicopter mode), or aft to the jet nozzle (for fixed wing mode). By directing thrust through the rotor tips, the CRW concept eliminates the need for a heavy and complex mechanical drive train, transmission and anti-torque system. The CRW's rotor is designed not only to spin during vertical takeoffs and landings but also to stop turning during flight and convert into a fixed wing to provide lift for high-speed forward flight. Aviation enthusiasts may have noticed that the X-50 designation was not the next in line. Boeing got the number out of sequence by special request because the X-50 designation is so fitting for the CRW concept – 50 percent helicopter and 50 percent airplane. Boeing Phantom Works built two X-50As reusing avionics, flight controls and Williams F112 engines from the X-36 tailless fighter demonstrators. The X-50A made its first hover test on 3 December 2003 at the Yuma Proving Grounds, Arizona. Unfortunately, the aircraft crashed on its third test flight at Yuma and was destroyed.

Artist concept of an operational unmanned Dragonfly. (DARPA)

The little X-50A demonstrators use many of the same systems and engines that were initially used by the X-36 tailless vehicles tested during 1997 and 1998. Unlike any other X-Plane in memory, the X-50A is being tested at the Army's Yuma Proving Ground. (Boeing)

The X-50 during its first hover flight on 3 December 2003. The aircraft flew for about 80 seconds, lifting off vertically from the launch site and hovering at an altitude of 12 feet above the ground. It then vertically landed. (Boeing)

GROUP PORTRAITS

A 21st Century lineup of X-Planes at NASA Dryden on 22 June 2000. From left, the NB-52B carrier aircraft, Boeing X-37, Boeing X-40A behind the MicroCraft X-43 mockup, and the Orbital Science X-34 and L-1011 carrier aircraft. (NASA Dryden photo by Tony Landis)

Those were the days. A group portrait of (mostly) X-Planes that includes the X-3 in the center and (clockwise from left) the X-1A, a D-558-I, XF-92A, X-5, D-558-II, and an X-4. (NASA Dryden Flight Research Center)

All of the same players, except the X-3, slightly rearranged. The skies over Edwards were a busy place during the 1950s and 1960s with a wide range of both X-Planes and prototype operational types being tested. (NASA Dryden Flight Research Center)

An all-Douglas lineup. In the foreground is the XF4D-1, which was visiting Edwards and joined the photo shoot. Behind it are (from left) a D-558-I, X-3, and a D-558-II. (AFFTC History Office Collection)

The NASA hangar on 27 June 1967. The X-15-1 is nearest the camera, followed by the X-15-3, and the ablative-covered X-15A-2. The M2-F1 and HL-10 are on the back wall. (NASA Dryden Flight Research Center)

Technically, only one X-Plane – the X-47 at left – but a nice collection of Northrop Grumman unmanned aerial vehicles. An RQ-4A Global Hawk is in the center, with an RQ-8A Fire Scout on the right. (Northrop Grumman)

A rare X-Plane group photo that includes a Bell X-2 (far right). Also shown are an X-4, XF-92A, X-5, D-558-I, and D-558-II. The Convair XF-92A was not technically an X-Plane, but certainly was testing new aerodynamic concepts. (AFFTC History Office Collection)

SLED TRACKS

So what do sled tracks have to do with X-Planes? Not much, really. But conceptually they are very similar, since both are used to evaluate and validate aeronautical theory, and both are intimately related to the High Desert around Edwards. Besides, there were some interesting photos that would not otherwise be published. So here is a non-inclusive look at sled tracks and the things that ride on them.

After Chuck Yeager broke the sound barrier in the X-1 on 14 October 1947, scientists and engineers knew that an airplane could safely fly faster than the speed of sound. But could a pilot bail out at such speed and survive? That was a question that had to be answered quickly because the first supersonic fighters were already being designed. It was certain that the wind blast on leaving the cockpit could dislocate limbs and break bones. There also would be rapid – almost instantaneous – deceleration, subjecting the pilot to very high G loads. Some scientists thought the human body could endure no more than 18 Gs, far less than would be experienced during a supersonic bailout. The Air Force assigned flight surgeon Lieutenant Colonel John Paul Stapp to find out just what a human could endure. Under Stapp's direction, Northrop built a 2,000-foot rail track on North Base at Muroc Army Air Field. A rocket-driven "sled" would accelerate to nearly 1,000 mph. Toward the end of the track, scoops beneath the sled would dig into a pool of water, stopping the sled in just over a second, simulating the deceleration of a high-speed ejection. This is the original Gee-Whizz sled on the North Track in 1947. (AFFTC History Office Collection)

Early passengers were dummies. At the end of one run, the safety harness broke and the dummy plunged through a one-inch wood windscreen, sailing 700 feet across the desert. In December 1947, Paul Stapp began riding the sled at increasing speeds. By May of the following year, he had rocketed down the track 16 times and withstood a force of 35-g's during deceleration. So much for the 18-g limit of human endurance. This is Stapp on the sled during November 1950. (AFFTC History Office Collection)

If the water did not stop the sled, there was this device to keep the sled and its occupant from sailing off into the desert. Basically it consisted of two large wheels with a cable strung across the track. The sled would snag the cable, and hydraulic brakes in the wheels would slow everything down to a stop. Pieces of this system still survive and were visited by Paul Stapp during 1992 (below). The "fastest man alive" died in his home on 13 November 1999 at age 89. (above: AFFTC History Office Collection; below: Christian Ledet)

The Navy operated a rocket sled track at nearby China Lake, California. This is a Navy Snort seat ejection being tested on 9 January 1958. (AFFTC History Office Collection)

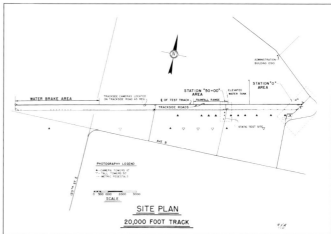

There was a need for a longer and more sophisticated facility, so plans were drawn up for a 20,000-foot track to be built near South Base where the majority of testing was being done. The photo at left shows the South Base sled track. (AFFTC History Office Collection)

Used sled lot at the South Track on 28 June 1956. (AFFTC History Office Collection)

Full-scale test of a Grumman XF-10F-1 Jaguar tail. (AFFTC History Office Collection)

A bomb shape being tested at the South Track. (AFFTC History Office Collection)

F-106 ejection seat test sled on 20 April 1960. (AFFTC History Office Collection)

F-104 tail flutter test on 10 February 1956. (AFFTC History Office Collection)

F-104 downward ejection sled (fuselage is upside down). (AFFTC History Office Collection)

B-58 escape capsule stability parachute test run #21-15 on 7 December 1960. (AFFTC History Office Collection)

Conceptual F-104 ejectable nose capsule run #6 on 7 December 1962. (AFFTC History Office Collection)

X-15 escape system run #3 on the South Track on 30 June 1958. (AFFTC History Office Collection)

Windblast sled during the final X-15 seat run on 14 March 1958. (AFFTC History Office Collection)

F-107 ejection system test run. The dorsal air intake presented a worrisome problem. (AFFTC History Office Collection)

The scoop on the bottom of the sled that was used to slow things down at the end of a run. (AFFTC History Office Collection)

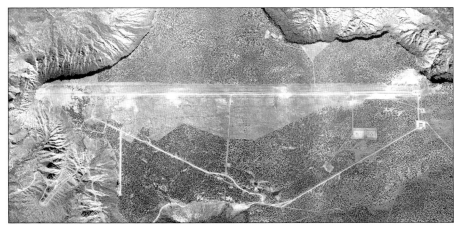

There was another sled track at Hurricane Mesa, Utah. This one was on top of the mesa (shown the photo at right), and some tests propelled objects off the track at high speed into the valley below. This is the facility on 2 July 1958. (AFFTC History Office Collection)

DESIGNATION SYSTEMS

When talking of X-Planes, many people assume that all research aircraft are issued official "X" designations. This is not strictly true.

First, it must be understood that there are two uses for the "X" in a military designation. Until recently, the military services would order prototype and service test aircraft prior to mass producing a design. The experimental aircraft normally carried an "X" prefix to their normal designation. Hence the XB-52. The service test examples would carry a "Y" prefix, resulting in the YB-52.

The other use for "X" is the one this book deals with. In this case "X" is the only letter in the designation and means "special research." (When first used in the 1940s the "X" simply meant "experimental.") This category was first used by the Bell X-1 in 1947 and was subsequently assigned to all Air Force aircraft dedicated to basic research. The number behind the "X" was simply a sequential count of how many designs had been designated. A letter suffix (A, B, etc.) tracked different variants of the basic design. Therefore, the X-7C is the third variant of the seventh experimental aircraft.

Prior to 1962 the Navy maintained its own designation system, and did not participate in the "X" series. This is why the Douglas D-558s simply used their company model numbers throughout their careers.

To further confuse matters, between 1947 and 1962 the Army assigned its own set of designations. Related to this book, the designation "VZ" was assigned to vertical takeoff and landing (VTOL) research vehicles.

While we are on the subject of vertical takeoff aircraft, it should be pointed out that several different terms have been used for these vehicles. In fact, the same aircraft has frequently been described using multiple terms. At times the terms have meant the same thing, different things, or similar things. In particular, the terms are: vertical takeoff and landing (VTOL), short takeoff and vertical landing (STOVL), and vertical/short takeoff and vertical landing (V/STOVL).

In 1962 the Department of Defense standardized the designation systems across all the military services, and "X" was retained for special research aircraft.

So this book covers the official "X" designation, both before and after 1962, as well as the Army "VZ" designation. I have also covered some "XV" aircraft, which are not, technically, research aircraft but rather prototype operational vehicles. However, in reality, all "V" aircraft except the AV-8 Harrier (and now, the V-22 Osprey) have been research aircraft. The "A" in the AV-8 designation signifies an "attack" aircraft.

Interestingly, the Harrier's designation is confusing since there had already been a "V-8" assigned. In 1963 the Ryan Model 164 Fleep was designated XV-8. The prototypes of the Harrier – P.1227 Kestrels – were tested under the XV-6 designation (after having briefly been called VZ-12 by the Army), so logically the production Harriers should have been AV-6s. The Navy, however, thought this would be confused with the Grumman A-6 Intruder, and also wanted the Harrier acknowledged as an attack aircraft. The next "A" designation was A-8, so the Harrier became the AV-8, ignoring the fact that the next "V" designation would have been V-12. It is all very confusing.

For a complete explanation of the military designation system, its history, mistakes, and rationale, please visit Andreas Parsch's excellent web site at:

http://www.designation-systems.net/usmilav/index.html

In the meantime, just remember, it really does not matter all that much!